REPUBLICANS SELL GOOD CRAP

It's About Time They Clean Up Their Act

The Pessimistic Optimist

authorHOUSE®

AuthorHouse™
1663 Liberty Drive
Bloomington, IN 47403
www.authorhouse.com
Phone: 1-800-839-8640

First published by AuthorHouse   7/25/2011

ISBN: 978-1-4634-0410-9 (sc)
ISBN: 978-1-4634-0409-3 (hc)
ISBN: 978-1-4634-0411-6 (e)

Library of Congress Control Number: 2011908567

Printed in the United States of America

Any people depicted in stock imagery provided by Thinkstock are models,
and such images are being used for illustrative purposes only.
Certain stock imagery © Thinkstock.

This book is printed on acid-free paper.

Contents

PROLOGUE

"CIVIL RIGHTS WHORE". The first time I heard those three words over the public air waves, I really thought my hearing was defective. Those three words kept ringing in my ears until I heard them again from the same person on the same radio station, referring to the same individual. Call me naïve, but having just recently arrived in the United States from England, I had not heard such language used on either radio or television before. "Was this the norm in America"? I asked myself, and soon realized that this type of disgusting language was polluting the airwaves on a daily basis all over the country.

The big eye opener for me was that the main offenders were Republican politicians, analysts and radio and television talk show hosts. Even more glaring was the muted response from the Democratic Party. They were no match for the Republican talking machine. Apparently they were amateurs in this field and had no answer, which strengthened the Republicans' resolve to continue with their poisonous rhetoric that has affected so many of their gullible supporters.

Those three words kept gnawing at me, but they were the words of just one person. These words alone could easily make one shrug ones shoulders, roll ones eyes, and move on. But, realizing that using that type of rhetoric is the common practice of most Republicans, I decided to undertake this project in an attempt to document and highlight the words and deeds of the main offenders, by putting them all together in the form of a book. My problem was that I had never attempted anything like this before, so I decided to put pen to paper and have a go as it's been said that the pen (which I possess) is mightier than the sword, (which I do not possess).

I also decided that it would be appropriate to temper my anonymity with an autobiographical introduction before moving on to the perpetrators of this poisonous rhetoric. Hopefully, this will act as the catalyst that drives well thinking Americans to find an antidote for this type of poison.

Chapter 1

My Early Years

SEVERAL DECADES AGO, my mother Kathleen, a wonderful petite woman who reached the ripe young age of 100 in March of 2010, introduced me to mother Earth. The event took place in a little district called Skibo, situated in Portland, Jamaica's most beautiful and fruitful parish. Electricity and piped water had not yet reached Skibo, and the main form of transportation was the" foot-mobile".

The population of around 250 moved around quite easily, because thankfully they were all blessed with their own foot-mobiles. Of course there was the odd mule donkey and bicycle, owned by the well to do folks. Once in a while, a truck would deliver goods to the only shop in the area, which was owned by a Chinese couple who incidentally had a son born on the same day as me. If my memory serves me correctly, they owned the only battery operated radio in the district and it was a thrill to go there just to hear some music, or listen to a cricket test match between the West Indies and England or Australia.

There were two rivers in Skibo, the Mabesque River and the Spanish River. I don't know their sources, but they flowed in opposite directions, met at what we called the Blue Hole, and flowed as one for about two miles down to the sea. They were protected by law and was the source of our water for domestic use. I can clearly remember my brothers and me making several trips to the river with buckets to fetch water to fill the huge drum we had at home. But we didn't mind because it gave us a chance to do some fishing which we really enjoyed. Naturally we had to make our own fishing lines. For the rods we used what we called wild cane, to which we attached wires that we cut, and then meticulously joined together with links like those in a chain. That was the easy part, the difficult part was getting the half penny to buy the fish hook, and believe me it was difficult.

As a matter of fact we had to improvise a lot, and learnt to make a lot of things, which the kids of today know nothing about. We would use the rubber from the old tubing of bicycle wheels to make sling shots to shoot birds, and make things like chokies, fringes, and calabans to trap them. We made our own cricket bats from coconut branches, and tree trunks, our own gigs to spin at Easter, and our own kites to fly at Christmas. Speaking of Christmas, it's amazing to see the gifts that parents can afford to give their children today, and it's expected by the kids. We were well and truly satisfied with a balloon and some fire crackers.

We had one Government school in the district, and that's where our basic education began. The school was situated on a hill, and could not be accessed by motor vehicles. The house I lived in was situated at the bottom of that hill, and so it was a relatively short walk to school for me. The headmaster, Mr. McLaughlin and his wife were friends of my parents. He was in my opinion a great teacher who did not spare the rod if you misbehaved. I can remember him disciplining a boy for swearing, and as the boy held out both hands to be strapped alternately, Teacher Mc. would say after each stroke of a hand,

"You must not use indecent language".

The funny part was that the boy had obviously never heard the word "indecent" before, but was aware of "decent". After each stroke he kept saying,

"I won't use decent language, Teacher".

One day I overheard him telling my father that it was his 32nd birthday, and that you really become a man at age 32, which left me wondering if I would ever live to be that old. Unfortunately, Teacher Mc was a chain smoker and died of lung cancer a few years later.

Chapter 2

My Introduction to Politics

AT AN EARLY AGE, I heard my father telling my mother that he was going to meet with a Dr. Fagan who was visiting our District. He was representing the Peoples National Party (PNP) and running against Mr. Lynch the incumbent Member of the House of Representatives who represented the Jamaica Labor Party, (JLP), and had never been beaten in an election. The leader of the PNP (the equivalent of the U.S. Democratic Party) was a brilliant lawyer named Norman Manley. The leader of the JLP (the equivalent of the U.S. Republican Party) was a not so brilliant man named Alexander Bustamante, also known as "Chief".

He is reputed to have said to the people in a campaign speech,

"I will give you B R E D"

Someone from the audience shouted,

"You left out the "A" Chief", and he responded,

"I will give you B R E D A"

To my astonishment, the people still cheered. He was selling good crap then even though I did not realize it at the time.

Sad to say Dr. Fagan lost, and Mr. Lynch remained undefeated until he died. My father was very disappointed, and so was I for him. That was my political initiation, the beginning of my skepticism regarding Republicans, and my complete disinterest in politics.

My father was an employee of the Public Works Department, and was transferred to Port Antonio, the capital of Portland. (Incidentally, I recently read an article published by Audrey Marks, Jamaica's Ambassador to the USA, in which she said that in researching Jamaica she discovered that John Brown Russworm, the second black person in America to earn a university degree, was a Jamaican born in Port Antonio in 1799).

The move to Port Antonio was like a new beginning for us, now we had electricity, paved roads, many stores, and a lot more people. In the household were my parents, three brothers and two sisters. Soon to join us was a three month old cousin Junior, the son of one of my father's sisters. His parents left him with us while they went off to America. He was loved, spoiled and treated like a little brother. Mr. Nolan, a boarder who said his full name was Bertram Alvin Derrick Paul Leslie Roe Woodrow McKenzie Nolan, and whose ambition was to earn ten pounds (British pounds) per week in the next ten years, was so fond of Junior that he named his first and only son, Junior. At about age seven cousin Junior joined his parents in America, and as soon as he reached eighteen he joined the U.S Army and went off to Vietnam. Within a matter of weeks his head was severed from his body by a bit of shrapnel, and Junior was no more.

We all attended the nearby Government school which was thankfully again within walking distance. The headmaster just so happened to be my uncle -in-law, being married to my mother's sister. The first, second, and third year examinations were the three taken in government schools, and looking back I cannot think why when I sat the third year exam I chose to write an essay on "Election day in Jamaica", when I had two easier choices. Thankfully my effort was successful.

Not long after I was fortunate enough to attend a Secondary School. This was a boarding school also located in Portland, but also in an area without electricity. However the school had a plant that supplied us with electricity, but it was only turned on at nights for a few hours. Television had not yet reached Jamaica, and no one at school had a radio, so we got most of our news from the Daily Gleaner, Jamaica's main newspaper. I was aware that slavery existed in America and the West Indies, but I also knew that it had been abolished a long time ago. Each year we celebrated the abolition of slavery on the first day of August which was called Emancipation Day.

The Jamaican Motto is "Out of Many One People", so regardless of race, we all thought of ourselves as Jamaicans. One day a headline in the Daily Gleaner caught my attention. It read "Race Riot in America". My first thought was, why would people want to riot at the races, and "races" to me meant the ones we trained for on the playing field. However, after reading the article I realized that blacks and whites were fighting each other because of a difference in the color of their skin and something called "segregation", not being able to use the same water fountain, bathrooms, hotels, or go to the same schools. This was my awakening to the real danger in racism.

Jamaica, was under British rule, and had a very high standard of education. In the secondary schools there were two examinations, the Senior Cambridge taken at about age sixteen, and the Higher Schools taken at about age eighteen. Both exams were set and marked by Cambridge University in England. The equivalent of the Senior Cambridge in England was the GCE "O" Levels (General

Certificate of Education) and the equivalent of the Higher Schools, was the GCE "A" Levels. What has always puzzled me is the fact that in England you could take one or more subjects at "O" Levels and receive a certificate for each subject passed, but in Jamaica, Senior Cambridge involved a minimum of eight subjects, with English being mandatory. In order to receive a certificate you had to pass at least five subjects including English. If you failed English and got seven distinctions in the other subjects, you would have failed the whole exam and receive no certificate at all.

I guess mother England gave preferential treatment to some of her children, or to be frank, the adopted ones were the less favorable.

Jamaicans have always resisted slavery and racism. From the days when a group of slaves called Maroons escaped to the hills, and fought the British; to the Morant Bay rebellion led by Paul Bogle; and in the sixties when a white South African in a managerial position told an employee with whom he had a dispute, that he would kick his ass if he were in South Africa. He was fired immediately and sent back to South Africa. If I am not mistaken I think little Jamaica was one of the first countries, (if not the first country) to ban South African goods during apartheid.

My teenage years in Jamaica were full of excitement and adventure. I was always aware of the great rivalry between the two political parties, but still had no interest in politics, and in any case I was still too young to vote. Some of the adventure and excitement came in learning to drive with the real "Sputnik", the name given to a 1945 Hillman Minx car owned by my older brother. It became the most famous car in Port Antonio, maybe because rumor had it that once it got to know you, if you were tired or had too much to drink, all you had to do was start the engine, and Sputnik would take you safely home. Sputnik brought a lot of joy to a lot of people for a number of years, but eventually died of overwork coupled with old age.

Then there was the other type of adventure and excitement, which involved learning about the joys and pleasures of one of God's greatest creation, (women), plus the ups and downs of two of man's worst creations, (alcohol and cigarettes). Naturally, there was much more pleasure in learning about women, than alcohol and cigarettes. During this period I became a 20 per day smoker, and an occasional drinker.

One day in 1982 to be precise I went home, had my dinner, and as usual lit up my Rothmans, the brand I smoked at the time. I really did enjoy smoking, and to me a cigarette after dinner was most enjoyable. For some still unexplained reason after I lit that cigarette, I held it up and said out loud,

"This is the last cigarette I am going to smoke"

As soon as I was finished, I went over to a nearby closet in which I placed the rest of the cigarettes along with the lighter. I have not smoked a cigarette since then. That's why it's so difficult for me to understand why people who want to stop smoking waste money on hypnosis, patches, pills, and all manner of things that don't really work, when all it should take is a little will power.

I started really learning about women at my co-educational boarding school, but did not smoke or drink there. This was a Quaker school with very strict rules, and breaking any of them could lead to expulsion. However, that did not stop us from taking chances. It would take a whole book to tell of my experiences with these wonderful, yet complicated female beings.

Chapter 3

Life in England

GROWING UP, I always visualized myself going to the Norman Manley International Airport getting on an airplane and whisking off to England, the Mother Country. This dream became a reality at the start of what is now known as the "swinging sixties". This is where I spent the next 33 years, except for a six month spell in Canada.

In 1979 Britain elected its first female Prime Minister in Margaret Thatcher a Conservative, who in my opinion did more harm to Britain than any of the other Prime Ministers that served during my time there. Under her leadership, the pound went to its lowest against the dollar, unemployment went to its highest, and inflation went to its highest. She introduced the unpopular poll tax which caused so much unrest in the country, and worst of all she tried to privatize the health system. In one go, she increased prescription charges by 3000%, and taxed unemployment benefits. I later found out she was a Ronald Reagan copy cat and was really relieved when she was finally forced out of office, and gave up the idea of running for Queen.

Yet another reason for me to be wary of Republicans.

Did I see any racism in England? Of course I did, especially in the sixties and seventies. I can remember signing on at the Labor Exchange clerical section and being offered truck loading jobs. I remember blacks having to pay more for car insurance than whites. I remember the manager of a football club saying that as long as he was manager there would be no black player on his team, even if his name was Pele (black, and the greatest footballer ever).

I remember working with a bunch of guys where I was the only black. We were all pretty young and the subject of race never came up. One day we had two new additions to the crew, one black "D", and one white "F". The guy in charge of the crew "T" had car problems, and I decided to give him a ride home. On the way home we were discussing the performances of D and F (incidentally D happened to be a friend of mine).

His first words were,

"When a black man like D comes on my crew he has to prove himself to me"

"What about F"? I asked

T's shocking response was,

"Well he's white, isn't he? That's enough for me"

"Are you saying that because he is white he automatically knows what he is doing" I asked,

"Yea" was his reply

I was momentarily stunned, but quickly gathered my thoughts, pulled up at the next bus stop, got out of the car opened his door and without saying a word, he knew what he had to do. Get out.

Some youngsters knew how to use racism to their advantage, and profited from it, though illegally. A friend told me of an incident she witnessed in a chemist (pharmacy). She was paying for some goods she had purchased, when a young black kid walked in looking a bit suspicious. He went to one end of the store, and all eyes were trained on him. As she was about to leave a young white kid walked in and went to the other end of the store, and her eyes were the only ones that were trained on the white kid. She watched as he filled a bag he had with goodies, and calmly walked out of the store. The black kid then left, and joined up with the white kid a few yards down the road laughing in celebration of their well organized theft.

Then there were the derogatory questions with sometimes very appropriate answers. An English woman asked a Jamaican woman,

"Is it true that the people in Jamaica live in trees?"

The Jamaican woman calmly replied,

"Yes ma'am, and when the Queen comes to visit, we let her sleep in the biggest tree"

So yes, there was and still is racism in England.

Chapter 4

THE AMERICAN ADVENTURE BEGINS

AMERICA was not a place that I considered living, and nothing changed when I visited New York, the "Big Apple" for the first time in 1973. Friends encouraged me to stay, but apart from the size of some buildings, New York was quite similar to London in many ways. Brooklyn seemed similar to Brixton, and Manhattan was just like the West End. Furthermore, being an illegal immigrant was something that I would never consider.

However, in 1978 I visited Orlando, Florida with two friends and we all fell in love with the place. We decided that Orlando was where we would like to settle down, and on our return to England started making the necessary plans. My two friends had relatives who sponsored them, and got their permanent resident green cards within 2 years. It was December of 1993 before I got mine, but I did not end up in Orlando as planned, I spent the first year in New York, arriving 1994 on the day O J Simpson's wife and friend were murdered.

The Big Apple turned out to be more than I had bargained for, and I knew almost immediately that New York was definitely not for me. Sure I was used to the hustle and bustle of London, but in New York it seemed as if they wanted today's affairs completed yesterday. I can still remember getting off the bus and heading for the subway at what I considered full pace, only to be passed by others and made to look as if I were in reverse. It was like driving at 60 mph in a 50 mph zone, and being overtaken by everyone else going at 80mph and above.

I returned to England in August of 1995, and stayed there until August of 1996. I wanted to give America another try, and was encouraged by a friend to check out Atlanta, Georgia and that is where I ended up during the 1996 Olympic Games. I flew to New York and then drove down to Atlanta with friends.

We arrived in Atlanta at about 6:00 a.m. and decided to have breakfast at a restaurant. I ordered bacon and eggs, and was then asked if I wanted anything to drink, to which I replied "yes", and went on to order tea. Bacon and eggs arrived looking delicious, and then came my first unpleasant American surprise, a glass of iced tea. After thirty years of having a hot cup of tea with breakfast every morning, this was really a shock to me and some negative thoughts started to haunt me. I had now surpassed the half century mark in age, and convinced myself that this time I would make it work, but soon began to wonder if I was young enough to make the necessary adjustments to fit into this new world, this new state, this new society.

Now I had to learn this new foreign language called Georgian English, drive on the right instead of on the left, and remember that a dual carriageway is now a divided highway. I would find out that what is legal in one State may be illegal in another, and police officers could be approached even though they wore guns. If I visited a doctor, I would be asked about my insurance before I was asked about my problem, and if I visited a hospital, I would later receive a bill. I would have to establish some form of credit, because no credit was the same as bad credit and would be hazardous to my existence. I would also have to get used to the idea that here in America football the world's most popular team sport is called soccer, while "sock em", America's most popular team sport is called football. I decided to stay and face the challenges.

In the weeks that followed I soon realized that unlike London, public transportation was not available in many areas, and it would be necessary for me to get a car. Someone informed me of a nearby auction, and so one evening I went and bought an old Chrysler. As I was driving around one day trying to familiarize myself with the area, I switched on the radio, flipping from station to station, and stopped when I heard someone letting off steam in language that I did not know was allowed to be aired on the radio. Yes, those infamous three words. I was flabbergasted. It turned out to be a man called Neal Boortz on WSB radio. This was my first experience of a Republican's abuse of Americans right to free speech, but I soon found out that there were many others like him. I also learnt that they refer to themselves as comedians, without realizing that they, and not always what they say, are comical.

My wife of 32 years was here with me in Atlanta. She was a nurse and never got over an experience she had. After being accepted for a job it was discovered that her blood pressure was above normal. She was sent to a nearby hospital where she spent about an hour until they got it back to normal. A few days later she got a bill for $350.00. Armed with the knowledge that there would be no charge had this taken place in England, it was not long before she decided that America was not for her, and returned to England. I visited England on several occasions since then but knew I would not return to live there. My wife on the other hand was not willing to return to America, so in 2002 we divorced. I am now a US citizen and eligible to vote. I had only voted once before and had no intention of voting again, because I still had no interest in politics.

Chapter 5

My Political Awakening

ON THE EVE OF THE 2004 Democratic Convention I heard that someone by the name of Barack Obama would be the keynote speaker, and that he was a very dynamic speaker. I was not very keen, but watched anyway and found this amazingly brilliant young man deliver one of the most inspiring speeches that I have been privileged to witness. I was so impressed that my very first words after he was finished were,

"We just heard a speech from America's first African American President"

Then on that cold winter's day in February, 2007 Barack Obama, the Junior U.S. Senator from Illinois announced his candidacy for the Democratic Presidential nomination, my interest in politics was ignited, and I have been more interested ever since. Let me just say I still know little or nothing about the subject, and it is not my intention to try and solve America's political problems. I am only trying to write about the things I have seen and experienced; things I have read about; things I have been told and things I have heard on radio, and television. The main focus however, is on the disgraceful behavior of some Republican politicians, commentators, analysts and talk show hosts.

Nothing in my past prepared me for my political epiphany into the world of U.S politics.

With Hillary Clinton the former First Lady and now U.S. Senator from New York in the Democratic presidential nominee race, no one (but a few like me) thought this Junior Senator had any chance of winning, but as time would tell, with overwhelming odds against him, he proved the non-believers wrong. He has since gone on to beat the Republican presidential nominee, Senator John McCain in the presidential race and is now the forty-fourth and first African American President of the United States of America.

These Republicans do not like a smart Democrat, more so if he's black, so in trying to denigrate him, they have labeled him the most liberal President of all time, and have attached such a stigma to the word "liberal" that Democrats seem to try and disassociate themselves from it. That prompted me to turn to my dictionary to confirm the definitions of these three words.

Conservatism:

> A political philosophy based on tradition and social stability, stressing established institutions, and preferring gradual development to abrupt change.

Republicanism:

> Primarily associated with business, financial, and some agricultural interests, and is held to favor a restricted governmental role in social and economic life.

Liberalism:

> A political philosophy based on progress, the essential goodness of man, the autonomy of the individual,

and standing for the protection of political and civil liberties.

We cannot ignore the emergence of the new Tea Party, and so I gave them my own definition.

Tea Party:

An organization initially formed with good intentions, but has now been usurped and over-run by a bunch of right wing racists, whose job is to carry out the orders of their wealthy sponsors. They now have the support of once moderate Republicans, and together they will use any means necessary to thwart the progress of President Obama and the Democratic Party.

Based on these definitions Democrats should be embracing the word "Liberalism" rather than running away from it, but Republican politicians, analysts, and radio and television talk show hosts are expert propagandists. They are a rare breed with the unique ability to deceive their supporters with such outrageous lies, even "mice with fully functioning human brains" (a Republican quote) would find difficult to accept, yet their supporters do.

Chapter 6

THE SELLING OF GOOD CRAP

THE BEHAVIOR of some Republican politicians and their supporters, are reminiscent to that of a drug dealer and his client I once saw in a movie, where the client after sampling some of the drugs he was about to purchase from this dealer, remarked,

"Man, this is *Shit*"

The dealer gleefully replied,

"Yea, but it's *Good Shit*"

The client handed over a large sum of money to the dealer, took the drugs and went on his merry way, happy in the knowledge that although he bought *shit*, the dealer had convinced him that it was *good shit*, and that was good enough for him.

I am convinced that drug dealer was a Republican, because only Republicans can convince people to knowingly buy crap on such a regular basis, and willingly return for more.

This is the mentality of Republican leaders, they take rumors and lies that serve their purpose, repeat them over and over through various channels like FRNN (Fox Republican News

Network) and WSB radio. Their supporters eventually buy all that "*Good Crap*", and keep coming back for more of the same, which they always get from the unlimited supply of their "dealers".

"Republicans sell Good Crap"

A considerable number of once moderate Republicans have joined ranks with the Tea Party and together they have one objective, which is to destroy President Obama at all costs even if it means destroying the Country they claim to love so much. These Republicans have something in common with the terrorists, they both hate this President. Just imagine Republicans in some States are talking about secession. I cannot recall a time in American history when one man was hated by so many from one party because of the color of his skin. Few will admit it for obvious reasons, but it is the absolute truth.

"Republicans sell Good Crap"

He has provided the necessary documents to prove he was born in Hawaii and his birth was documented in two Hawaiian newspapers soon after. Yet Republican so called "birthers" have been able to convince a large number of people that he is not American, but was born in Kenya, that he is also a muslim, a communist, and the anti-Christ. If he were born in Kenya, his mother being American would have had no problem in having him become a naturalized American citizen, enjoying all the rights that Americans have, except he could not run for the office of President of the USA. This was in 1961 when racism was still at its peak in America, and blacks had difficulty getting jobs of any real importance.

"Republicans sell Good Crap"

The thought of a black president was not even a remote consideration by anyone, but birthers strongly believe that his parents looked into their crystal ball and saw their African-

American kid wanting to run for this coveted office, so they smuggled him unnoticed into the country and had him registered as being born in Hawaii, an American citizen by birth. People who escape from institutions and wreak havoc among regular folks are almost always caught, restrained, and re-instutionalized, and so will the "birthers". Now, can we move on?

"Republicans sell Good Crap"

During the 2008 presidential campaign, and since President Obama's inauguration, racism seems to have shown its ugly face more often than it has done for a very long time. Thanks mainly to the Tea Party. The hate shown at their meetings through their banners, guns, and general bad behavior is unbelievable, but confirms what I have already said in my definition of the Tea Party. One of their statements that really grabbed my attention was,

"We want our country back"

I simply smiled to myself at such stupidity. It did not come from an Apache or Arapaho, a Blackfoot, Cherokee, Comanche, Crow, Kiowa, Mohawk, Navaho, Pawnee, Seminole, Sioux, Shoshone, or a member of any of the Native American tribes I have omitted, and they are the only ones with exclusive rights to such a statement. I saw no Native Americans at their rallies. All I can remember seeing were a bunch of middle aged white folks with racist banners, and the odd attention seeking blacks.

They sell Good Crap but,
Thank God they are in the minority.

Chapter 7

New Experiences

SO I HAD LIVED in Jamaica the land of wood and water, England the land where tyranny trembles and now reside in America the land of the free and the brave.

I am still idiosyncratically Jamaican, unavoidably British, and currently a "Jamerican".

I have not personally experienced any racism here in the USA but on one occasion came face to face with the type of disgusting behavior that African Americans had to face. On one of the walls in an African American doctor's office, was a framed letter which was the reply he got from a college to which he had applied to study medicine. It read,

"I regret to inform you that I am not allowed to accept applications from people of the negro race. Enclosed is your application fee."

I realize this was minor compared to the killings, beatings, lynchings and insults perpetrated on them, but it struck me to the very core of my being because I actually felt as if I were going through that experience. Then I saw the movie "Rosewood".

This made me start thinking about Affirmative Action, which I had heard of but did not fully understand. I soon found out that it was first established in 1961, an Executive Order 10925 signed by President John F. Kennedy, in an attempt to promote equal opportunity in government and educational settings. It was then superseded by Executive Order 11246 signed by President Lyndon B. Johnson in 1965, affirming the Federal Governments' commitment to promote the full realization of equal employment opportunity through a positive continuing program in each executive department, and agency.

Now correct me if I am wrong, for hundreds of years these employment and education opportunities were given exclusively to whites, without protests from anyone. That in itself was a form of affirmative action, but exclusive to whites only. This was just a revised version of affirmative action which gave those rights to minorities less than fifty 50 years ago, and Republicans want to take those rights away. African Americans are still being treated unfairly where jobs and education are concerned, and to take away affirmative action would make matters much worse.

What does it mean when the Governor of Ohio with an all white cabinet openly tells a black Ohio State Senator who offered help?

"I don't need your people"

Or, when a black woman is imprisoned for seeking better education for her child? It simply means that those Republicans would like African Americans to continue living the American nightmare that has plagued them for so many years, while whites only live the American dream.

Enough is enough. Leave Affirmative Action alone.

Chapter 8

THE HATERS

FOR THE FIRST TIME in its history the United States of America has an African-American President. Since his inauguration, Republicans, with one or two exceptions have said "No" to everything he has proposed. If he agrees with them that the world is round, they change their mind and say it is flat (their supporters would buy the *good crap*). If he agrees with them that one plus one is two, they change their minds and say it's eleven, and then have the audacity to accuse him of being a partisan (and their supporters would buy the *good crap*). Their aim is to do whatever it takes to make him fail. That has been their objective from day one to just say no to every thing he proposes.

There are genuine black and white "Obama policy haters", and they do have the right to disagree with some things, because that is what democracy is all about, but there are also black and white "Obama haters". It is my firm belief that the vast majority of white Obama haters are racists. They are completely pissed off that the White House is occupied by a black family and that they have access to Air Force One. It is driving them crazy, and so they show their hatred in any way they can. The obscene banners, nasty name calling, filthy language, comparison to Hitler, and guns at their gatherings is proof enough for me. This President with his calm, cool, and collective attitude, has not stooped to their level, and has handled the situation with dignity.

"Get over it, this is the 21st century"

The black "Obama haters" are a completely different story. I honestly think they suffer from a hereditary disease. Just like diabetes and alzheimers is passed on from one generation to another, so too was their disease passed on. It is commonly known as "self-hate". Their ancestors must have been the ones who helped the slave traders round up and capture their countrymen for money, the ones who informed on the slaves that tried to escape to freedom. They must have been the ones who fought with the Confederate Army in the American Civil War for the sole purpose of preserving slavery, because they might have been privileged to stay in the master's house, and the ones who opposed Martin Luther King and others in their fight for civil rights. They are well paid by their white bosses, because they can do their bosses dirty work by vilifying other blacks without their bosses being accused of racism.

They remind me of a fact based movie I saw, where a young Jewish boy grew up hating himself and his religion so much, that when he was old enough, he became a member of this anti-Semitic, neo-Nazi organization, where he mercilessly wreaked havoc on his own people. He got his well deserved tragic comeuppance, and so will the black Obama haters.

"Father, forgive them even though they know what they are doing. They just cannot help themselves".

President Obama against all the odds has been able to sign a new Healthcare Bill into law, which provides health care to millions of Americans who had none before. He accomplished a feat that eluded previous presidents who tried but were unsuccessful. Republicans fought vigorously against it, successfully selling their "death panel" lies to quite a number of people. They have even voted to repeal it now that they have the majority in the House. Like I said before, Republicans are experts at what they do. They have convinced millions that people in Europe and Canada are dissatisfied with the health care system in their respective countries, and run to America for treatment (if they can afford it) whenever they have health problems.

"Republicans sell Good Crap"

As one who lived in England I can categorically deny this. As a matter of fact, independent surveys show that over ninety percent of people in England are satisfied with the National Health Service which provides health care to all permanent residents. It is free at the time it is administered, but paid for by general taxation. Prescriptions have a fixed charge of about $10.00 to $12.00 (depending on the exchange rate) per prescription. Children under 16 years old and adults over 59 years old get prescribed drugs free, with exemptions for people with certain medical conditions like cancer, and those on low incomes.

"Pensioners and poor people of America I ask you, what is so bad about that system?"

Surveys also show that the death rate in the U.S.A is higher among males at 29% and females at 23%, than in England and even higher among blacks. Now remember America is reputed to have the world's 'best' health care system.

"Is that really true?"

It should also be noted that England has a private health care system which may be acquired through private health care insurance, of which I am sure many Americans are not aware.

It is understandable why so many Americans are opposed to what Republicans have branded socialized medicine, because they have never experienced it, to know of its advantages. It has been ingrained in them all their lives that the government will take over their health care, when the truth is, government is only trying to stop insurance companies from ripping them off.

"Is that so hard to understand"?

Let me share with you two experiences I have had with this great health care system, one with insurance and one without.

With insurance - One night I felt this severe pain in my side. I called the emergency room of a nearby hospital only to be informed that my pain was not an emergency.

"Why not"? I asked.

The shocking answer was,

"We only consider things like broken legs and death to be emergencies"

"I kid you not"

The following morning I went to a clinic where I explained the problem I was having. After several visits co-payments and tests, they concluded that I had a muscular skeletal strain. They explained what it meant but said they could not treat that condition there and would refer me to someone who could.

"I kid you not"

Off I went to this new doctor. The receptionist said there would be a charge of $100.00 which I promptly paid. Ten minutes later after a five minute examination the doctor confirmed that I did have a muscular skeletal strain and prescribed pain killers.

"I kid you not"

Each day the pain got worse and so I went back to the clinic. Eventually they decided that it was necessary for me to go to a hospital. They sought the approval of the insurance company who denied their request, because they could not see any good reason for me to be hospitalized.

"I kid you not"

Two days later I was paralyzed with pain. It was so bad that I could not move any part of my body. An ambulance was called and I was rushed to the emergency room of a hospital for my non-emergency problem. There I was given a pain killing injection and thankfully the pain soon subsided. A nearby specialist was called in. He entered the room looked at me and said,

"Make sure you have good insurance, it's going to come back again.

He then left the room and I never saw him again.

"I kid you not"

X-rays of my lower back had been taken on my arrival, and later that day I was given an epidural. I spent the night at the hospital and was allowed to return home the following day. The hospital apparently had problems with the insurance company, because the bill was sent to me. The fee for the specialist that suggested "make sure you have good insurance" was $425.00.

"I kid you not

Without insurance - I made an appointment to see the urologist, and was told I had to wait three weeks. The day finally came, and off I went to keep my appointment. After I told the doctor about my problem, he said there were two tests that had to be done because that was the "ONLY" way to find the cause of the problem. He went on to explain what was involved in the tests, at the end of which I asked,

"Doc what will these tests cost, because I have no insurance?"

There was a moment of silence, then with this look of shocked disbelief he asked,

"You have no insurance"?

"No doc" I replied

He simply reached for his pen, wrote a prescription and handed it to me and said,

"Try this and come back and see me in four weeks"

Because I had no insurance the absolutely necessary tests were no longer necessary.

"I kid you not"

It would have cost me $120.00 to have that prescription filled. It so happened that I had planned to go to England about three weeks later, so my son made a doctor's appointment for me. On my arrival I went to see my doctor. He took a urine sample, had it tested, and then wrote me a prescription which I had filled at no cost, and the problem went away.

"I kid you not"

Based on those two experiences I was now convinced that the insurance companies controlled America's health care system, aided by the support of the politicians they have in their pockets, and will use any means necessary to try and stop the government from intervening to make changes to help the millions of uninsured.

It is ironic that the Republican Party having been formed with good intentions by anti-slavery expansion activists in 1854 has now been usurped by such a large number of *Good Crap* sellers.

SO ALLOW ME to have some fun with the main culprits who sell Good Crap.

I have noticed that in a number of cases the spelling, meaning, or sounding of part, or all of their names, and also by adding or subtracting a few letters to or from their names, may tell us why they behave the way they do.

Let's start with the "Odd Couple

John MCain the last Republican to run for President

and,

Sarah Palin his running mate and the first female Republican who thought she, and not him was running for President.

Chapter 9

John McCain

NO ONE CAN DENY the fact that John McCain has served his country very well as a Naval Aviator. When the Vietnam War started he volunteered for combat and flew several missions over North Vietnam before he was shot down and taken prisoner by the North Vietnamese. After his release he returned home to a heroes welcome. His service and bravery earned him several medals including the Silver Star and Purple Heart.

The five and a half year celebrated POW has now advanced to a twenty four year POWer seeking Republican Senator. There is no doubt that his ordeal in prison greatly affected him. It must have had a delayed reaction which is now surfacing, because based on his behavior he does not seem to know whether he is coming or going. He has made two failed attempts to become President. In his 2008 campaign, he made the biggest political blunder in his career. In a moment of madness to which there was no method, he chose the politically dumbest female in the Republican Party to be his running mate. He opened up a can of worms and out stepped Sarah Palin who eventually turned the tables to make him her running mate.

It's sad to see a once celebrated war hero become so disillusioned, bitter, selfish, and confused. Disillusioned because he was unable to become President so he could bomb, bomb, bomb Iran and keep American troops in Afghanistan indefinitely. *Bitter*, because he suffered such a humiliating defeat by Barack Obama, and cannot get over it. *Selfish*, because he said he knew how to capture Osama Bin Laden, and did not reveal his method to George Bush during his 8 year reign, or to the current President.

Confused, because he doesn't know whether he is a maverick or not. Confused, because at the start of what turned out to be the worst recession to hit the country since the thirties, he said the fundamentals of the economy were strong. Confused, because of his insistence that voting for the man responsible for the recession 90% of the time, was the right thing to do. Confused, because he told the people of Pensylvania that the Obama supporters were saying some nasty things about them, and he agreed with the Obama supporters. Confused, because he said Al Qaeda was on the run in Iran. Confused, because he said Vladimir Putin is the President of Germany.

Confused, because he called on "Joe the Plumber" to speak at an election rally when he was not even in the building. Confused, because he said he had never requested pork, when he did. Confused, because he said he never supported amnesty when he did. Confused, when he thought he could fool anyone by showing up at a MLK birthday celebration during the 2008 election campaign to apologize for his resistance to that holiday, not having attended the previous year, or since then. Thankfully the American people were spared the four years of agony his victory would have caused. This was due to his disastrous campaign, highlighted by his string of senior moments, and the eventual breakdown of the "straight talk express".

Most people work very hard to earn letters after their names, but he has spent a lifetime trying to put letters before his name, and definitely deserves them. "CONFU"John McCain.

"Live with it, you earned it"

Chapter 10

Sarah Palin

AT THE TIME of her selection by Confujohn McCain to become his running mate, she was the Governor of Alaska, a relatively unknown person to the inhabitants of the other forty nine States. I am sure he was in his confused state of mind when he chose her, but I believe he would have done anything necessary to become President, and in his confused state decided that somehow she would help to get him there

What a disastrous decision. Sarah the savior arrived, and was given the super star treatment, drawing huge crowds with every appearance she made. She was new, she was exciting, she was original, and she was from scandal free Alaska, not scandalous Washington. Was this the super woman the Party had been waiting for? After all, she had injected new life in the Party, and people traveled miles just to see and hear the party's new Messiah.

Then something interesting happened. She was interviewed by a journalistic super star in Katie Couric, and all hell broke loose. She has made it necessary to change the term "dumb blonde" to "dumb brunette", because she proved how empty she really was. Other interviews proved just as disastrous, and so she stopped giving them to genuine journalists, and turned to Fox News for consolation. But she still managed to hold on to a lot of supporters, and continued helping to steer the "straight talk express" over the cliff. Fortunately for her she came out of the accident virtually unscathed, and went back to Alaska a triumphant woman.

She may be politically dumb, but financially smart, and realized that with her new found fame her financial opportunities were infinite. As governor of Alaska she could not explore these opportunities, and so she had to make a decision between her fickle love of her job, and her unconditional love of money. Surprise, surprise, money won. Money is the "be all and the end all" in America, and there is nothing wrong with grasping these opportunities when they present themselves. What was wrong in her case was that she had to quit her job in order to achieve this goal, and lied about her reasons for doing so. She claimed that one of her reasons was,

> "To fight for all our children's future outside the Governor's office"

Everyone knows it's about fighting to secure her own financial future. Did she really say?

> "I hate this damn job"

Having quit her job I do not think that the full title of Governor should be bestowed upon her, and suggest from this moment on she should be known as the "ERNOR" of Alaska. What really puzzles me is how quickly the Ernor became one of the Republicans biggest earners. Apparently this woman is one of the best sales persons ever to wear the name Republican because in a matter of months she out sold the best in her Party, and there are some very good salesmen in it.

She definitely has the gift of the gab, and smiles and laughs convincingly so people believe she is laughing with them rather than at them, winks convincingly so some men believe she is winking at them rather than conning them. She lies convincingly so people believe she is telling the truth rather than warping their minds, and before long she has millions of mesmerized but victimized followers who don't even realize they are victims. To top it all she makes millions for her efforts, her victims get nothing, and all she is doing is putting a new spin on how to sell the same old Republican crap. Is it legal? I guess so because it comes under the guise of free speech, which is used by some to con so many.

With her new found wealth she should first buy an English dictionary, and hire an elocutionist. He or she will certainly teach her how not to "cackle" whenever she opens her mouth. She should then take a course in political science, which may take her about five years. By then she should be able to give sensible answers in an interview and conduct herself properly in a debate, by answering the questions asked, and not the ones she thinks she should be asked.

The year 2016 will be upon us, and by then she may no longer be the politically dumbest female in her party. She could then seek the Republican Party's nomination for President. If by some miracle she should succeed, she may have the privilege of running against a great female politician in the person of Hillary R Clinton. Obviously she won't stand a chance, but it would be good TV with millions watching to see how she wasted five years, and still made a fool of herself.

Apparently, Republicans love to reward ignorance because they have elected someone with a degree in political ignorance as the new face of their party. I am convinced she eats the wrong end of the moose on a daily basis, and this may be the reason she spouts so much verbal diarrhea. Remember she actually got sponsored by a sump pump manufacturer. A third grader simply asked her what was the job of the Vice-President, which is the job she was applying for, and she could not give a sensible answer. Little did this innocent child know she had presented her question to a forty year old political first-grader.

Sometimes people say things without really thinking, just to get cheap laughs. She calls herself a hockey mom, and says the difference between a hockey mom and a pig is lipstick. If that's true, then does that mean that when she and the converted hockey moms remove their lipstick, they become pigs?

Just asking

She also claims to be a Mama Grizzly, and Mama Grizzlies she says, know when danger is lurking, so they stand on their hind legs and growl to protect their young ones. Where was Mama Grizzly when dangerous Levi came along? With her vast experience and association with animals, she should have warned her daughter that humans, especially women have a better chance of survival, if when approached by predators they remain in a vertical position rather than a horizontal one. Also, now that she has another coming of age teen, instead of trying to be cute by crowning herself with these ridiculous titles, and gallivanting around the country uttering those onomatopoeic screeches which are so hazardous to the ear, she should use this opportunity to rein this daughter in, and prevent her from perfecting the art of personifying vulgarity.

I imagine the Ernor's optician is doing really good business, because he must have provided the spectacles that allowed her to see Russia from where she lives, maybe not, because she is unable to see the newspapers or magazines she reads which may account for her confusing an "f" with a "p" in her use of the non-word 'refudiate'.

Was this malapropism? Definitely not. Was it a mistake? A

slim probability. Could it just be "Palinism", the new synonym for ignorance?

You decide America

For someone to suggest that the late great William Shakespeare would have been delighted to "refudiate" is surely laughable, because I can hear him shouting from his grave,

"All the perfumes of Arabia cannot sweeten that big mouth of yours, Sarah"

Before her dramatic surge from insignificance to prominence, I understand she had never left the shores of the United States of America, but why should she if she is able to see countries of other continents from her home. Maybe that is how she gained her vast experience in foreign policy and national security. It could also be her argument that she is Governor of Alaska, and Russia is her next door neighbor or Confujon's suggestion that no one knows more about energy than her?

Does she realize how much harm she has done to senior citizens by her selling of "*Good Crap*", scaring them with her "death panels" and "killing grandma lies"? The deadliest form of terrorism is that inflicted by groups like Al Qaeda, but people who inspire fear are also regarded as terrorists, and that is exactly what she is doing to America's senior citizens. How low is she willing to sink to gain political capital? The answer is simple. She will do whatever it takes. To make matters even worse she has defended Dr. Laura in her use of the "N" word and her racial explosion, when a woman in an interracial marriage simply called her radio show for some help on how to deal with racial comments from her husband's friends.

She must have cast some kind of a spell over her fanatical followers, because when she said the best way to commemorate the anniversary of "nine eleven" was to do so with Glen Beck, (the man who hates 9/11 families) they forked out up to $200.00 to join them.

After the tragic shooting incident in Tucson, I watched and listened to the comments made by the various talk show hosts on MSNBC, and without exception they all said that Sarah Palin was NOT responsible for the tragic events that took place, and all the politicians I've listened to have also agreed. Yet on the day they chose to mourn their dead she came out with "guns" blazing accusing the media of blaming her for the tragedy and acting as if she were the victim, while one of the real victims, Congresswoman Gabrielle Giffords was laying in a hospital bed in critical condition from the injury caused by a bullet that went through her head.

How ironic that Gabrielle Giffords now the victim, was the one who initially pointed out that Sarah Palin had targeted her district by putting cross hairs on a map over her district, and that there would be consequences. That's what most people were referring to, but as usual the Ernor showed how cold and selfish she was. It was a Republican who summed it up correctly when he said she was like an iceberg with pieces falling off daily. Based on that description, the hotter the political climate, the sooner she will disappear, and the country will be much better off.

One would assume that after so many blunders she would at least lay low for a while, but not her. True to her word she will not shut up, but continue to make a complete fool of herself by exhibiting her ignorance, which she did on Fox News (where else).

Soon after the President's State of the Union address, she suggested that the collapse of the Soviet Union in the nineties was a result of their investment in the space race of the fifties. She went on to say she wanted a "spud nut moment", but she should really be careful what she asks for, because with the amount of nuts now showing up in the Republican Party, she will have not only a "nut moment", but a "nut era". My suggestion to her would be, "If you have nothing to say, say it loudly".

Confujohn started this nightmare and he should try to awake the country from it. One of the new Republican phrases is "man up", so he should man up and start repairing the damage he caused by simply admitting his selection of this Ernor / mamma grizzly/ hockey mom/ truth distorter/propagandist, was a huge mistake. Admit he screwed up, like he did on the David Letterman show. It could go a long way in helping to repair his tarnished image. After all she disrespected him when she was in Hawaii wearing a cap with his name conspicuously blocked out.

She disrespected all Republican politicians when she responded to the question of whether or not she would seek the Republican Party's presidential nomination, by saying that she would have to first look at the lay of the land to see if there was any one Republican enough in the Party to do so.

He may even agree with me when I say,

"The writing is on the wall (or in the hand)" and. "America will soon wake up to the terrible truth that they have no PAL in selfish Sarah".

"Isn't that a shame"?

Chapter 11

Rush Limbaugh

HERE WE HAVE THE GODFATHER of the Republican radio talk show hosts. The self appointed leader of the Republican Party no one in the Party dares to offend for fear of suffering his wrath. He became the "Incredible Bulk" after a gammon radio experiment as a radio disc jockey went terribly wrong, and now uses his power to wreak havoc on those who disagree with him. He is reputed to have more followers than any of his colleagues in the same business, and like a pied piper, he leads, and they blindly, but happily follow him to the land of Limbaugh lies, deceit, fear-mongering, sexism, and racism. Once there, he sells them Good Shit, controls them like puppets on strings and feeds them with his brand of distorted grandiloquence.

I once had the unfortunate experience of witnessing someone having an epileptic attack. It was very scary, because he fell to the ground, started shaking violently, and I did not have a clue as to what was happening to him. Fortunately, his guardian who had seen it all before was there. She took control of the situation and was able to allay the fears of all who had gathered around him by explaining that he must have forgotten to take his (prescribed) drugs, and that he would be back to normal in a matter of minutes.

Where am I going with this you may ask? Well, every time I see clips of Limbaugh behind the microphone on his radio show or making a speech at a Republican gathering, I am reminded of the incident because he always behaves as if he is having an epileptic attack. This was particularly evident during his 2009 CPAC speech, but his audience reveled in it. The more erratic he got the louder they cheered. The big difference is that he is always upright, hopefully taken his drugs, well aware of what he is doing, but shaking and gesticulating much more. Does this mean that his drugs bring on his daily epileptic attacks?

Let's hope he obtained them legally.

These are the occasions on which he throws out more racist remarks than the KKK. Of course he would not publicly admit to being a racist, even he is a bit smarter than that.

He off-handedly says,

"Barack would be a tour guide in Honolulu, if he were not black"

He gleefully uses his favorite name for the President,

"Barack, the magic negro"

He dismisses the first African-American female billionaire,

"Oprah has a lot of money because she is black"

If it is his opinion that their success was gained because they are black and not because they earned it, then he is a racist but wants us to believe that he believes in a color blind society.

If it is his opinion that they ought to change black history month to black progress month and start measuring it, then he is a racist but wants us to believe that he believes in a color blind society.

If it is his opinion that a black caller should take the bone out of his or her nose and then call him back on his radio show, then he is a racist but wants us to believe that he believes in a color blind society.

If it is his opinion that all composite pictures of wanted criminals resemble Jesse Jackson, then he is a racist but wants us to believe that he believes in a color blind society.

If it is his opinion that quarterback Donovan McNabb got a lot of credit for the performance of his team that he did not deserve, because the media has been desirous that a black quarterback do well, then he is a racist but wants us to believe that he believes in a color blind society.

If it is his opinion that African-Americans in contrast with other groups are left behind because they have been systematically trained from a young age to hate America through a movement headed by Jeremiah Wright and the Obama's, then he is a racist but wants us to believe that he believes in a color blind society.

If it is his opinion and that people should not donate to the relief funds for earthquake ravaged Haiti, then he is a racist but wants us to believe that he believes in a color blind society.

His racism has no boundaries, because it covers all non-white races. The disrespectful behavior he showed to the Chinese President by mimicking him is proof of that, and the threats received by Mr. Lee the California State Senator, who asked for an apology are a direct result of Limbaugh's disgusting behavior.

Based on his statement claiming that feminism was established so as to allow unattractive women easier access to the mainstream of society, he can be branded as sexist. He says his cat has taught him more about women than anything in his life and for the sake of his current wife, I hope I am wrong about my next prediction. If he chose to gain his knowledge of women from his cat, then marriage number four could be a catastrophe and number five may not be far away. Number five would have to be even braver than the previous four, but money can be very persuasive. Just the same all four deserve medals.

Go see a shrink

The BP oil rig explosion caused the worst oil leak the world has ever had. The Gulf and its surrounding shores were polluted and thousands of people were affected physically, psychologically, and financially. This was a time to unite, this was a time to put politics aside and try to find a solution. Not so, because this Republican "wacko" in an effort to score political points has the gall to suggest that "environmentalist wackos" deliberately blew up the well to stop off-shore oil drilling. His scientific solution being, the ocean will take care of it on its own.

He repeatedly disrespected the President by calling him among other things, a "jackass", and maybe that's what he thinks of all black people. He was way out of line, and people who live in glass houses should not throw stones, because he looks like someone who still has a jack up his ass, which may account for some of his erratic and disgusting behavior.

This man has "rushed" to the top of a multi-million dollar money tree. He is sitting on a "limb" and moves further out each day. It will eventually break and he will tumble down. If he does not explode, hopefully he will bounce all the way to Costa Rica (where he claimed he would live if Barack Obama got the Healthcare Bill passed), if they will have him, and if at all possible, via China.

"It's only a matter of time"

Chapter 12

NEAL BOORTZ

BOORTZ HAS MILLIONS of followers on his radio program, many of whom are not aware of the fact that he has asked them not to place any credence to anything he says, because he is only an "entertainer" selling good shit. Hence they take him at his word and believe everything he says. He thinks he is a wise-acre, but as far as I am concerned he isn't even a square chain. He once accused Al Sharpton of name calling and said he would not have him on his show because he (Boortz) does not engage in that type of name calling. Now, that's hilarious because this man stands head and shoulders above every one that I can think of with a doctorate in name calling.

Naturally he saves the nice names for himself, Mighty Whitey, (which I think he cherishes most, and I'm a bit surprised he left out "Bwana"), Talk Master, America's Rude Awakening, Mouth of the South, High Priest of the Church of the Plain Truth, Equal Opportunity Offender", and for his wife, "The Queen", and for friends like Sean Hannity another Republican talk show host, "Baby Jesus".

The nasty names however are given to minorities, the poor and the uneducated. He refers to civil rights leaders Al Sharpton as

"Al the Liar Sharpton" and Jesse Jackson as "Jesse the Slogmaster Jackson" saying they are both "race warriors". Some Katrina victims he calls "Worthless Parasites", while homeless people are "Urban Outdoors Men". An innocent nine year old he calls a "Worm Farmer", and Cynthia McKinney a "Ghetto Slut".

"Civil Rights Whore", his name for Jesse Jackson was the one that really stood out probably because of its hypocritical nature. Here is a man who sits on his posterior five days per week raking in millions of dollars for calling people nasty names. Doesn't that make him and his like-minded colleagues the biggest 'talk show whores' in the universe?

"I think it does"

He is completely anti-government, and suggests that the government take the people's money by holding a gun to their heads. He claims that Social Security is a Ponzi scheme just like the one Bernie Madoff ran, and wonders why its implementers are not in prison like Madoff. He should be very careful about what he asks for, unless he's forgotten that pimping and prostitution are also illegal.

He certainly has a smart, way of exhibiting his racist remarks and behavior with the hope that no one notices. Both he and Sean Hannity publicly voiced their differences over the Terri Schiavo incident and although they disagreed, the discussion ended amicably. I have heard Belinda Skelton (a producer on his radio show) disagree with him on several occasions, and each time they basically end up laughing about it. Twice I heard the late Royal Marshall (another producer) disagree with him, and on both occasions he gave Marshall the disloyal treatment, rather than the royal treatment, by simply losing his cool. In my opinion his response on both occasions was insulting, and embarrassing.

On one occasion Royal dared to disagree with him about

finding weapons of mass destruction in Iraq and was stopped in his tracks. And if my memory serves me right, he (Royal) was silent for the rest of the show. Incidentally, if Boortz was Sadaam's lawyer and if Sadaam's only crime was the possession of stockpiles of "wmd's", but based on the evidence found "wsh" (just a whimpering Sadaam Hussein) and he could not get the charges dropped, then it's understandable why he no longer practices law.

The other occasion was when Marshall came out in support of then Senator Obama, and was silenced by Boortz's response. With his white colleagues he disagreed without being disagreeable, it was the complete opposite with Marshall. Imagine an African American having to work in an environment where his boss is constantly and unfairly trashing the first African American President. Every day a barrage of nasty name calling, possibly to increase the ratings for his show, and not being able to respond for possible fear of losing his job in this terrible economic climate. It would be enough to stress any one out.

I always wondered why he would always dismiss with noticeable annoyance anyone who dares to bring up the subject of racism on his show, and realized it might have something to do with conscience. That's assuming he has one. He is the type of person who will tolerate black people who work with him as long as he is in charge. They should always be subservient, and hold positions of less importance, that way he can say he is not racist because he has black friends and colleagues. He reminds me of a white workmate I once had.

We got on really well and I regarded him as a friend. He was the happy go lucky type, in his mid fifties. He came in to work one morning looking really sad, not even saying his usual good morning to everyone. I waited until we sat down for our break, before I asked him what was wrong. He told me that his daughter who had only been married for a year had run off with another man. Having only recently been married myself, I told him how sorry I was, and did my best to console him. There was silence for about two minutes, and then he said,

"You and I get on very well, don't we"?

"Yes" I replied.

"So you know I have nothing against black people?"

"As far as I know", I replied.

That's when he showed his true colors by saying,

"What really pissed me off is that she ran off with a black man"

I summoned all my will power so as not to burst out laughing, and my only response was,

"Really!"

Here was a man who would not have minded the break up of his daughter's marriage if she had run off with a white man. This is what is called hidden racism the type I believe is practiced by the "B" man. I can't help but imagine a scenario where he discovered that his beloved daughter was dating a black man, (probably named Marshall). She would be struck from his will, Marshall would lose his job, and the title of his new book would be "Guess who's not coming to dinner".

One of his latest theories is, now that Barack Obama is President, the NAACP is no longer necessary. He says they are just a bunch of "race pimps", and need to go away. That's how true racists think that we now have a black President, so racism is over and done with. Not so "B" man. It is more rampant now than it's been for a very long time, and your rhetoric encourages it.

That may explain why I have him under the category of "white Obama hater". No one on radio or television to my knowledge has disrespected this President more than him. The barrage of nasty name calling is a daily occurrence. Everyone knows that the Clintons were not his favorite people, but I do not recall him ever calling President Clinton any of the nasty names that he has showered on this President. When it comes to the President of the USA, there is a line that should not be crossed. He has never crossed that line before by calling any of the other Presidents he disagreed with an idiot, but he has now, and brags that people should get used to it. Why? This President is African-American, and he knows he will get away with it.

Free speech?

Where is the protest from the Michael Steeles and Ron Christies of the Republican Party? Silly question eh? Everything this President does is criticized by him. Maybe he needs to be more critical of some of the companies whose services and goods he so adamantly promote on his show, like the one I am about to mention.

The tenant of a rental property called to inform me that his water had been turned off because it was gushing from a leaking pipe which had created a large hole in the front lawn. I left home about 10:30 that morning, and headed towards the property. On my way there I turned on my radio and heard Mr. B advertising his favorite plumbing company which he said would respond within one hour. Great, I thought he's doing something good for a change.

The situation was urgent, because it's no fun having to cope without water. I stopped my car, wrote the number down, and called the company. A female voice said they could have someone there by 3:30 p.m. that afternoon.

"I was just listening to the Neal Boortz show and he said you would respond within an hour" I replied.

"Hold on for one minute, ok sir someone will be there by 12:30pm"

"Thank you" I said, and she hung up.

The plumber did arrive on time, surveyed the situation and suggested that at a cost of $300.00 he needed to dig a hole to see what type of pipe had originally been installed. I was looking at a gaping hole in the lawn, and wondered if this plumber needed to see Palin's optician.

I saved myself $300.00 by getting a flash light and pointing it towards the hole so he could see the pipe. I was then told the existing pipe was no longer in use and would have to be replaced by copper, or PVC now being used. After making some calculations he informed me that the labor and material cost for the copper would be $2400.00 and for the PVC, $1800.00. I said I thought those prices were a bit too high, after which he suggested he could do it privately for $1200.00. I told him I would think about it, so he gave me his card and drove off. I called another plumber who had been previously recommended to me, and had the job done for $600.00 the following day.

"That's a fact Mr.B".

It's been rumored that he is one of the Republican's (calls himself a Libertarian) chief scientific experts on global warming. He probably has a degree in this field also, which makes him conclude that humans have no effect on global warming. Of course that decision could have been influenced by lobbyists rather than his expertise, but who knows or who cares. The point is, he professes to know more than the thousands of real scientists in the body known as the Intergovernmental Panel on Climate Change, who all agree that people are contributors to global warming.

You go smart ass"

When he gets bored with his own disgusting rants, he turns to bragging about his piloting and golfing skills, and when he is bored with that he tries to promote his book on Fair Tax which I have not read, but just based on the fact he had a hand in it, I know it should be called the "Fear Tax".

I am sure he has himself some very good health insurance, which should serve him very well in his condition. He has given the "BS" phrase new meaning by substituting "Bull" with "Boortz", which makes him full of "It", and the only way for him to get rid of "It", is to have an "Aboortzion".

"Enjoy the pain"

Chapter 13

GLENN BECK

I UNDERSTAND this is a man who said that for fifteen years from age sixteen, he was high every day on alcohol and drugs, and was eventually saved by Alcoholic Anonymous, and the healing power of Jesus Christ. To invoke Jesus' name in his so called "turn around", equate God with gold, and then spout his daily distorted, seditious, racist, vitriolic, fear mongering, misinformed statements is blasphemous, but hiding behind Christianity is the Republican way of pandering to their base.

Having been diagnosed with "Attention Deficit Hyper-activity Disorder" whatever that means, he must have replaced the alcohol and drugs with something even more dangerous, which is the cause of his current condition, "over exposed attention seeking sycophantic disorder". Maybe he is inhaling too much of his own breath and drinking an excessive amount of "mad puss piss" (a Jamaican terminology) for him to utter some of the nonsense that comes out of his mouth. He was probably better off with the drugs and alcohol.

Some people need a gimmick to express themselves and for him it's a black board and sticks of chalk to sell his Good Shit. With this he sets out to educate his fanatical followers about the facts of "politricks". His teachings, which have been very successful, include the art of running smear campaigns against people like Van Jones (Obama Administration); how to stop federal funding for organizations he dislikes, like Acorn; how to decimate church congregations by encouraging them to leave if they hear the term "social justice" used. In his one track mind this means "naziism" and communism" and of course his favorite scam; how to invest in his gold buying and selling scheme.

It took him he says, one year to start hating 9/11 families, because they were always complaining, he was sick of them and that they should shut up. Now he is against the building of a Muslim community center near "ground zero", because it will upset the 9/11 families he hates so much. Got it?

"Way to go Glenn it makes a lot of sense"

One of his latest scams was his so called "restoring honor" rally, held at the Lincoln Memorial on the forty seventh anniversary of Dr. Martin Luther King's famous "I Have A Dream" speech. He claims it's to pay tribute to military personnel, and those who embody the nations founding principles of integrity, truth, and honor. Great if it were true, but I think he was paying tribute to his fans who are the cause of his swelling bank account and the lap of luxury in which he now sits. His convenient and selective memory caused by his ignorance regarding the date of choice, which he said was coincidental, and divine guidance. His honor is probably the only one needed to be restored, but how can he restore something he didn't have in the first place?

Thousands of fans once cheered a lunatic named Jim Jones, and he eventually led 900 fools to their deaths. Now tens of thousands are cheering this con artist as he leads them down the road of no return. He said he has no intention of running for President. Of course not, he is much more ambitious than that.

The ill-fated preacher Jim Jones said to his followers,

"If you see me as your God, I will be your God"

And that is what Glen Beck wants to be to his followers "GOD", and they will let him because he really sells "Good Crap", and they love it.

"Violence is coming and it's coming from the left" says Beck,

But it's the lunatic right that's stomping on a woman's head, illegally arresting reporters, punching people, threatening to take out a reporter, and threatening to take up arms against the government, with him actually saying,

"You're going to have to shoot them"

Does this guy ever get anything right? Silly question, because he is the master at selling crap, and he has many gullible customers. Speaking of violence, I understand he wanted to have a captured terrorist shot without being investigated or having a trial. If he were as smart as he thinks he is he could easily have had it accomplished without any controversy at all, just by arranging for the terrorist to go hunting with Dick Cheney.

Does any one really believe that his apology for calling President Obama a "racist" was genuine, when less than twenty four hours later he said he did not want to retract his statement, but amend it. That's as false as Dr. Laura's apology for her use of the" N" word and then resigning from her job to find a venue where she could use it without criticism.

Quite likely he has now surpassed "Rush & Company" in the race for the title of "Male Republican Maniacal Supremacy", which is a coveted title among them. A "glen" is a narrow valley, so its not surprising Glenn Beck has turned out to be the narrow-minded twerp that he is.

This definitely qualifies him as "worst person in the world".

Chapter 14

Sean Hannity

NOW HERE IS ANOTHER very good salesman of the Republican product. His sales are from Monday to Friday every week, and can be found on TV at FRNN and on radio at WSB. He has a large devoted following that watches and listens enthusiastically, without ever challenging anything he says. I once heard President Obama say in a speech that he did not hate insurance companies, because they were in business to make money.

Just minutes after the speech, Hannity in his analysis said,

"I cannot believe the President said he hates insurance companies"

No one on the panel corrected or challenged his erroneous statement, but then again why would they if they all think alike. Maybe way back in 1808, Sir Walter Scott was thinking of someone like Hannity when he wrote in a poem. "Oh what a tangled web we weave, when at first we practice to deceive". This is what he does every day. He intoxicates his viewers and listeners with lies and innuendos, they take it all in and return daily for more, like hooked junkies returning to their dealers for another hit.

When everyone thought that Hillary Clinton was going to be the Democratic Presidential candidate, he started the "Stop Hillary Campaign", and actually said a few nice things about Barack Obama. As soon as Hillary lost, he started the "Stop Obama Campaign". He would have been a very successful gravedigger, because he devoted a lot of time trying to dig up some dirt on Senator Obama, in an effort to bury him. After coming up empty handed, he discovered Bill Ayers, whom he gave to Sarah Palin, and hence the start of the "Pal-ing around with Terrorists" debacle.

Like so many of his Republican colleagues, he has this fanatical fascination with Sarah Palin, and seems to love having her on his show. Based on the questions he asks and the expression on his face when she is there, it's easy to conclude that his reason for having her on is not to interview her, but just to view her.

"Good luck"

Consider this hypothetical improbability, or better yet, impossibility.

Hannity – "President Palin (doesn't even sound right) what programs would you cut to reduce the deficit"?

Palin – "Any of 'em, all of 'em that comes before me"

Hannity – "How would you go about protecting the United States from its enemies?"

Palin – "That would be up to my Vice President John McCain, who I'm sure would just go ahead with my permission (got to show him who is in charge) and bomb, bomb, bomb them all"

Hannity – "Are you talking about conventional bombs?"

Palin – "If by that you mean nukes, then the answer is, Yes"

Hannity – "Is it true that members of your family have been up to Canada to take advantage of their health care system, which you now call socialized health care?"

Palin – "Well you see we were poor then, but now that I am a millionaire we don't need such things in our great country"

Hannity – "Explain to the viewers what you meant when you said people should take up arms"

Palin – "They have to understand that "arms" is just another word for hands, so they should lift up their hands and vote"

Hannity – "How would you go about solving America's unemployment problem?"

Palin – "Just send more jobs to China"

Hannity – "I don't see how that would help to reduce unemployment"

Palin – "Borrow my glasses Sean. The unemployed would eventually have to go to China to find work. And, it would also help with the immigration problem"

Hannity – "Why were you so easily fooled by the hoaxer who called you up and pretended to be the French President?"

Palin – "That was no hoax. It was him, but you know the

Democrats had to spread that rumor to try to make me look bad"

Hannity – "That makes sense. My final question is what do you think of the media and journalists in general"?

Palin – "Sean, I've studied journalism, I have a degree in Journalism, and with my vast knowledge on the subject, I have so much to offer, and I would like to help them but they won't let me. Present venue not included, because you guys are almost as good as me"

Hannity – "Thank you for spending the last hour with me, please come as often as you can because this has been the best hour I have had on TV, and you were really marvelous".

It's really amazing that a so called experienced host like him does not realize that he is doing her more harm than good with such "petty views". In 2008 he did one of the most stupid and ridiculous things in his entire controversial career. I have concluded that this behavior can only be due to one of two reasons.

1. His love for himself which borders on narcissism, and should give his wife a reason to be jealous.

2. He believed the lie Boortz told him that he (Hannity) is "Baby Jesus". Because Jesus tried to Christianize the world, big-headed Hannity decided he was going to "Hannitize" America.

"Keep on trying, the whole world is watching you make a fool of yourself"

Chapter 15

DICK CHENEY

THIS IS THE MAN who was convicted of DWI at age 21, and arrested for the same offence the following year.

This is the man who received five deferments when he was eligible for the draft during the Vietnam War.

This is the man who voted against a bill over riding Reagan's veto of the bill to impose sanctions on South Africa's apartheid government. His reasons being, sanctions almost never works and they might end up hurting the people. What he really meant was, they would end up hurting white minority South Africans. Just tell me how sanctions could hurt the black majority whose suffering could not have been made any worse than it already was.

This is the man who voted against a congressional resolution calling for the release of Nelson Mandela. His reason being Mandela supported the African National Congress which he viewed as a terrorist organization with interests hostile to America. The Tea Party thinks the current Administration has views hostile to America. As a Tea Party supporter, does he think this Administration is a terrorist organization?

This is the man who provided most of the selective information that led to the unnecessary war in Iraq claiming the lives of over four thousand Americans, hundreds of allied troops, and tens of thousands of innocent Iraqis. He still tries to convince people that Sadam was somehow connected to 9/11.

This is the man who is alleged to have leaked the information on the identity of Valerie Plame, who was at the time a covert CIA employee. If someone can be arrested for "wiki-leaks", then so should he for "wicked leaks".

This is the man who allowed a friend to take the fall for him. This is the man who mistook his 78 year old acquaintance for a quail and shot him (accidentally it's said) in the face, neck, and upper torso. He may want to consider moving his next hunting trip to Arizona's third congressional district where he will find a real live "Quayle" running around uncontrollably chirping in his tone deaf voice. He won't be hard to find as he is the only one there described as Quayle, white, lawyer, with wings that need clipping."

"Be careful, aim for the wings only"

This is the man who supports water boarding and enhanced interrogation techniques (which he does not regard as torture) for captured "terror suspects".

This is the man whom I hope practices what he preaches, even though that would not justify him asking a colleague to perform a sexual act on himself.

This is the man who has no regard for public opinion.

This is the man some regard as the most powerful and influential Vice-President in history.

"Wrong"

This is the man I regard as the most powerful and influential "President of Vice" in history.

"How does he sleep at night?"

Chapter 16

Michael Steele

HERE COMES THE FIRST African-American ex-chairman of the Republican National Committee. At first he wanted to be a catholic priest, and spent three years studying to achieve that goal, before he changed his mind and went into politics. With hindsight he should have chosen medicine and hopefully would have developed a cure for his current affliction, "human foot and mouth disease". It is quite amazing that every time this man opens his mouth, he sticks his foot in it within seconds. It got so bad that even members of his own party were critical of him, and wanted him gone. On more than one occasion he had literally been asked to resign, but refused to comply.

He called for the overturn of Roe vs. Wade because in his opinion it was wrongly decided.

"foot in mouth"

He suggests that the Afghanistan war is a war of Obama's choosing, and not something the United States had actively prosecuted or wanted to engage in.

"foot in mouth"

He says "the $7.8 billion stimulus (which has saved the car industry, and created and saved millions of jobs) is a reckless and wasteful pork-laden spending spree".

"foot in mouth"

He publicly ridicules a woman by suggesting her behavior would get her on television when all she did was to speak of her mother's death, caused because she could not afford some of her prescription chemotherapy medication, and believed that every one in the country should have access to good health care.

"foot in mouth"

He calls civil unions, "crazy"

"foot in mouth"

He says, "Embryonic stem cell research compares with experiments carried out by the Nazis during the holocaust"

"foot in mouth

He says, "We're cooling, not warming. The warming is part of a cooling process. Greenland is covered in ice and is named Greenland for a reason"

"foot in mouth"

He also said,"Senator Ted Kennedy's letter read by the President was a political tool"

"foot in mouth"

It's now obvious that "human foot and mouth disease" can lead to insanity, because some of his remarks are the ramblings of a mad man. He tried in vain to get re-elected, but failed miserably when his colleagues aimed their feet at him, connected at an orifice much lower than his mouth, and sent him back to his position of irrelevance. Now that he has been kicked out of this job, he will definitely surface again, because his main reason for running for any office is to "piss off Democrats he has not yet pissed off".

"foot in mouth"

After he was criticized for comments he made about abortion, he said "he sought God's help so that he absolutely did not have to go out and kick that person's ass", but I bet it also crossed his mind that he no longer had ex brother in law Mike Tyson to back him up.

Only once while he was chairman of the Republican National Committee did he say something meaningful. He said Rush Limbaugh was an entertainer whose entertainment was incendiary and ugly. We all know what happened after that. Limbaugh chastised him, saying he was not fit to lead the Republican Party. Instead of standing his ground, he crawled back to apologize saying he was sorry to upset Rush, and people who wanted to make Limbaugh the scapegoat and bogeyman were wrong, because he was a national conservative leader. It's so sad that a man with a name like Steele can so easily be associated with "cotton balls".

There is a regular clip on television showing him and others on stage with the "Ernor", where he is showing more teeth and clapping harder than anyone else. I would not be surprised if he had blisters on his hands.

Apparently he has not got the message, because he is still running around trying to convince himself that he is one of the "boys", not realizing that he was really used, as the Republican Party's answer to President Obama, a dismal lack of judgment on their part. He was the Republicans black heavyweight, but they gave him the Jack Johnson treatment. The promotion made him think that he was indispensable, but colleagues have made it clear that the Party is already in trouble, and they need to provide a much better quality "STEELe" to have any chance of trying to help America compete on equal terms with the other steel producing countries of the world.

"Sorry mate, but it's all over for you"

Chapter 17

Bobby Jindal

HE IS THE FIRST Indian-American Governor in the country, and at thirty six the youngest at that time. Republicans had very high hopes for their young exciting newcomer. There was even talk of John McCain selecting him as his Vice Presidential running mate in 2008, which turned out to be just talk anyway. But .anything suggested by Limbaugh becomes a big talking point. Then it happened…

He was given the impossible task of responding to President Obama's address to a Joint Session of Congress. I need not comment on his response because it was so pathetic. However, whenever I hear the name Bobby Jindal I picture in my mind's eye a man walking down a corridor, who appeared to be staggering as he approached the microphone. He did not look like a Republican. He looked like a Publican who had just raided his private stock and consumed the contents of a bottle containing a 100% proof liquid that sounds like the first three letters of his surname", "GIN". Where is the law when they are needed? He should have been arrested for "SUI" (speaking under the influence).

"You have blown your chance"

Chapter 18

The Seven Deadly Sinners
Keyes, Christie, Thomas, Caine Williams,
West, Blackwell

Alan Keyes

HE IS THE EPITOME of a "black Obama hater". This man Alan Keyes has run for President three times and got whipped, for U.S. Senator three times and got whipped. On five occasions he was beaten by white men but showed no hatred for them. He was severely trounced by Barack Obama (now President) refused to congratulate him on his victory, and now hates him with a passion. In his 2008 bid for the Republican presidential nomination, after being ignored by the members of his own party, he switched to the Constitution party who in turn also snubbed him. So he tried to form his own party, which of course failed miserably. Every one in his party stays away from him including then Governor Jeb Bush, who refused to meet with him to discuss the Terri Schiavo nightmare.

There is always an exception to the rule, because President Reagan probably out of pity gave him a place in his administration.

But there was a price to be paid. He threw black South Africans under the bus, by supporting Reagan's policy of not imposing economic sanctions on apartheid South Africa. What kind of African American would stoop so low?

In one of his many idiotic outbursts, he suggested that slavery meant, guaranteed shelter, guaranteed clothing, guaranteed food, and that is what liberals and leftists want Americans to aspire to, which simply means becoming slaves on a government plantation.

He also said he does not want this country to go back to the condition in which his ancestors sadly found themselves. Black liberals he said are using the" moral capital" used by those who fought for civil rights as a political tool.

Let me address these points. He (Keyes) was using the "moral capital" as a financial tool to line his pockets when he paid himself $100,000 per year from campaign funds and refused to pay campaign expenses. Based on my definition of "black Obama haters" his ancestors thrived in those slavery conditions because they were probably a part of the problem. As far as what slavery meant, is he really saying that slaves were guaranteed shelter, food and clothing?

Let me help him fill in the blanks he omitted. Slaves were regarded as animals and so they were guaranteed inadequate shacks to live in, guaranteed rags to cover their bodies, guaranteed slop to stop their hunger, and if that's what he meant then he is correct. But they were also guaranteed beatings, guaranteed hangings, guaranteed stud farms, guaranteed rape of their women and innocent little girls, guaranteed break up of families, which guaranteed that sometime in the future a nincompoop like him would eventually surface.

I understand he (another "birther" idiot) is involved in a

law suit to verify whether or not Barack Obama is a legitimate President. The NAACP should seriously consider filing a lawsuit against him for trying to impersonate a black man. It should be so obvious to him by now that he is the laughing stock of all politicians, so he can throw away his "KEYeS" because they will never open any political doors for him.

He's earned ENVY - The desire for President Obama's traits, status, abilities, and situation

Ron Christie

NOVEMBER 2010 on the release of a book by former President George W. Bush, Christie appeared on MSNBC's Hardball, and bragged about his proposed meeting with the ex President. He then lost his cool, (as he always does when challenged) in his defense of Bush's insistence that the Iraq war was justified, because we were not attacked again. Maybe he needs to visit Sarah Palin's optician and have his glasses changed, so he can see more clearly.

In the years between the first Gulf war and the start of the current Iraq war, how many Americans were killed by Sadaam or terrorists operating out of Iraq, Ron? None.

Since Sadaam Hussein's death, how many Americans have been killed by terrorists operating out of Iraq Ron? Many more than was killed by the 9/11 attacks, not to mention the thousands that were maimed.

Yes Sadaam killed his own people, but now America can be blamed for needlessly killing tens of thousands of Iraqis. So Mister Defender of the perpetrators of an illegal war, with your new glasses can you see what I'm saying. Just imagine that your bosses did every thing the same way, except invading Iraq, thousands of deaths would have been prevented, billions of dollars would have been saved, and America would not have been attacked by Sadaam. He had no weapons of mass destruction, and was basically a coward who would not have the balls to launch an attack on the United States, knowing full well what the consequences would be.

It got worse when he went on to defend Limbaugh's racist "driving Miss Nancy" taunt by calling it satire, and got really mad because someone said it was racist. His behavior is probably understandable anyhow, because they are all afraid of Limbaugh, and he was probably pooping in his pants at the thought of Limbaugh chastising him as he did Michael Steele.

I think this former Dick Cheney aide, and now Republican strategist not only has a vision problem but also a serious name problem. His name should really be Tom, and he should have lots of nieces and nephews who call him every minute of every day, as a constant reminder of what he really stands for. But his name fortunately or unfortunately for him is "Christie" and he tries to use it to his advantage by making these regular television appearances, always pretending to know more than anyone else each time by conveniently forgetting that he has an "ie" at the end of his name.

He gets FALSE PRIDE:-His excessive belief in his own ability that interferes with his recognition of the grace of God, because he acts as if he is God.

Clarence Thomas

I HAVE ALWAYS believed that if the "Browns" and the "Goldmans" were black, O J Simpson's trial would not have been called the trial of the century, and so many books would not have been written about it. He would still have his home and his

69

trophies, he would still have his celebrity status, and he would not have been imprisoned (although his stupidity contributed to the residence he now occupies). By the same token there is no doubt in my mind that Clarence "doubting" Thomas would not be a member of the Supreme Court of the United States of America if Anita Hill were white. Most people believed her story, but those who mattered, did not.

Now two decades later his ex girlfriend has broken her silence and started talking, because she says, she is not afraid anymore. She agrees with Anita Hill's accusations against him and suggests he was an alcoholic, a bully to his child, a pornography fanatic, and that his court decisions are personal, whereby he tries to punish his enemies, and reward his friends. She says, his enemies are people active in civil rights and people who have criticized him, while she named Rush Limbaugh as his friend. If he really regards Limbaugh as a friend then it's easy to conclude that he needs psychiatric help.

This woman has no reason to lie, so just stop and think about this self hating Republican making decisions that affect the lives of every American. Imagine what the right-wing Party would do with this revelation if he were a Democrat. More than likely they would have found a way to remove him from the Supreme Court.

Why would someone in his position say "Government cannot make us equal"? In my opinion that's a really stupid statement made to pacify his white colleagues, because all black people already know that God created all men equal. To my recollection African Americans have never asked the Government to make them equal, they have only asked to be treated equally, and there is a big difference.

He deserves LUST - His alleged inordinate craving for the pleasures of the body.

Herman Caine

HE CALLS HIMSELF the 'Herminator", and says he is prayerfully considering a 2012 bid for the GOP presidential nomination. It seems as if his prayers have been answered, even though he might have decided that No means Yes, or to be more precise, as most Republican politicians do, distort the truth, even when it comes from the Almighty. Because now that he has decided to enter the 2012 Presidential race, he says President Obama is a master of rhetoric and deceptive language, (the very same thing he is trying so hard to achieve) and he also says that any white candidate who runs against President Obama will be up against the race card, but he Caine takes the race card off the table.

Now think about that, the 'Herminator" was putting the race card on the table before he sought the nomination with the intention of removing it after he seeks the nomination. *Sounds crazy?*

The statement that really hit a nerve is the one where Caine says,

"The biggest challenge of the GOP will be to educate people (which they have already done with lies and scare tactics) because the President and Congress are leading this country towards socialism and communism".

And then he boasts, "There, I said it"

"Yes you said it".

Are you going to follow in the footsteps of that man named Joseph McCarthy, who had the same warped thoughts as yours, and set out to destroy any one who could even spell the word communism?

Because of McCarthy's policies, Martin Luther King and other civil rights leaders were harassed, persecuted and even murdered. Those are the leaders whose sacrifices paved the way for a man like Caine to be able to climb to the top of the "mountain" and be able to even consider running for President. Continue down that road Mr. Herminator and see where it leads. Try taking the country back fifty years by reintroducing "McCarthyism". He says he is "ABC" American Black Republican. Maybe he really meant "ABM" America's Black McCarthy. Sounds crazy?

Yes, this man has entered the 2012 Presidential race.

I say, "Run Herman run, go make a fool of yourself"

Maybe just maybe if through some form of madness the Republicans nominated him, he could choose Neal Boortz as his running mate and reverse roles with him, whereby Boortz would be subservient to him for a change. *Sounds crazy?*

Why is it that when some people (in this case a black man) reach the top they forget the people who are still trying to get there, and even the suffering of their parents? Maybe that's why he makes such stupid comments about the signs people brought to the Tea Party Rallies like,

> "People brought signs that denigrated the image of the President, but not because he is black, but because they did not like his policies"

That's like saying the KKK burnt crosses on black peoples lawns not because they were black, but because they didn't like them living in houses. *Sounds crazy?*

At a Tea Party rally he asked KKK members to raise their hands, and no one did. He asked members of any white supremacist organization to raise their hands, and no one did. He then asked all the people who were patriots of the U.S.A. to make some noise, and everyone cheered. Big deal. He should go into an asylum, and ask the inmates to raise their hands if they are insane, and no one would, or go among a den of thieves and ask them to raise their hands if they thought they were criminals, and no one would. Then ask them if they loved this great country and there would be an overwhelming yes, even from the nuts. *Sounds crazy?*

If he thinks that failure to enforce the current immigration laws is just negligence by the Federal Government, why on earth didn't he mention it at any time during the eight year reign of the previous administration, why wait until now? *Sounds crazy?*

It's not at all surprising that he supports the Arizona Immigration Bill signed into law by Governor Brewer. Nor is it surprising that he agrees with the Hispanics he clams have called him up to express their disgust at what the current administration is doing, in giving a free pass to all who are here illegally. Not at all, because he is just like them, they have betrayed their race and he has betrayed his. *Sounds crazy?*

He claims that he is more hated by blacks, now that he is running for the Republican Presidential Nomination, because they now regard him as a threat to President Obama. (*Laughable-egotism*). According to him, he will not return to the plantation – the plantation being the Democratic Party to which so many Civil Rights leaders belonged, and still do. Sounds crazy?

His supporters believe him when he says he is Crazy about the Constitution, Crazy about the Declaration of Independence, and Crazy about the United States of America. What they don't realize is that he may be just plain *Crazy!* As the ex-CEO of Godfather's Pizza, he should now be considered for a new title "Godfather of the Tea Party".

He is the GLUTTON - His inordinate desire to bite off more than he can chew.

Armstrong Williams

THE HOST of the television program "The Right Side" who tries to 'Strong arm" his way through life, has been alleged to have been paid $240,000, a large sum of money to promote the Bush Administration "No Child Left Behind" Law which he now claims to be bad judgment on his part.

It was bad judgment on his part that caused someone to sue him for sexual harassment.

It was bad judgment on his part to have such close ties to the well known segregationist Strom Thurmond.

It was bad judgment on his part to defend the behavior of Dr. Laura Schlesinger and her use of the "N" word in response to a woman's plea for help.

It is good judgment to brand him with the sin of GREED - His excessive desire for material wealth ignoring the realm of the spiritual.

Allen West

THIS NEWLY ELECTED Florida Congressman had to cut short his military career after it was alleged he threatened to kill an Iraqi he was investigating. He left the Army an organization formed to protect the country, and joined the Tea Party an organization that is willing to destroy the country in an effort to make this President fail. It's really not surprising to hear him tell supporters they could defeat his Democratic opponent by making him afraid to leave his home. Imagine an African American making such a statement, when not so long ago the KKK made blacks afraid to leave their homes. Joyce Kaufman the woman he wanted to be his Congressional Chief of Staff said that Jewish people voted for President Obama because they did not want to embrace being Jewish any more.

Allen West did not reproach her

Based on that assumption, did he join the Tea Party because he did not want to embrace being African American anymore? This woman did most of his dirty work for him by promoting the hate and fear needed to give him the votes he needed to win the election. She blamed undocumented workers for the pollution and disease that is destroying the environment in this country, knowing blacks were once blamed for the same things, and in some cases injected with the disease (syphilis) when they didn't have it.

Allen West did not reproach her

If they committed crimes she thinks they should be hung, knowing blacks were hung even when they did not commit crimes.

Allen West did not reproach her

She said if ballots didn't work bullets would, knowing that bullets were once used on some blacks when they tried to vote.

Allen west did not reproach her

This excuse for an African American knew all this, yet he embraced this woman and defended her behavior.

Yes, he definitely deserves SLOTH - Avoidance of physical or spiritual work.

Ken Blackwell

KEN IS WELL BLACK, but is in denial, and he is also accident-prone. He served in the administration of George H W Bush as Undersecretary in the Department of Housing and Urban Development. His office published the social security numbers of Ohio residents, which he said was an" accident", and then they "accidentally" published them again.

In his 2006 campaign his campaign workers "accidentally" placed flyers on the windshields of vehicles of members attending service at the Lord of Life Lutheran Church in Columbus two days before the primary.

He refused to withdraw the Diebold Election System when it was discovered to be faulty, and was found to "accidentally" have shares in Diebold, the company that makes the machines.

This man is hungry for power and recognition, and a hungry man is an angry man, which gives him.

ANGER - His strong feelings of antagonism; this leads him to reject love and opt for wrath.

Chapter 19

Michele Bachmann

HERE IS A WOMAN who says she bears a close resemblance to Nostradamus and also has regular conversations with God, whom she said told her to run for the U.S. Senate. She confirmed it was God, by fasting with her husband for three days. Apparently she was given a new set of commandments.

1. Thou shall not raise the minimum wage

2. Thou shall not have a clean energy and security act

3. Thou shall not believe in global warming because it's a hoax

4. Investigate Members of Congress for their anti American beliefs

5. Slit your wrists in opposition to health care reform

6. Do not complete Census forms because the Constitution does not require it

7. Consider a nuclear strike on Iran

8. Do not save the U.S auto industry

9. Be armed and dangerous to achieve your goals

10. Thou shall listen to no other but me the Savior of our Party.

Obey these rules and you will be welcome into the kingdom of "Bachmannism".

What a joker. She now seems to be a close associate of the "Ernor" and is probably a regular dinner guest, also eating the wrong end of the moose, which may account for her outlandish outbursts. Somehow she always appears aloof as if she is under a spell, which tends to suggest she is being punished for a fight she might have had with Christine O'Donnell.

"Bach" the man was a fantastic organist, and a musical genius, with whom she says she would love to have dinner.

"Bachman" the woman is a disorganized fanatic, who will eventually become seatless in her silly version of political musical chairs.

Now that she has decided to run for President, she is beginning to sound like a broken record with her repetitive sound bite "Barack Obama will be a one-term President". This is an achievement she will never accomplish and an accomplishment she will never achieve. It is estimated that 5% of Americans are stupid, and so if she miraculously gets the Republican nomination, then the 5% stupidity was grossly underestimated and confirms without any doubt that they all belong to the Republican Party.

Chapter 20

Siamese Twins (Coulter and Ingraham)

Ann Coulter

A TRUE REPUBLICAN FREAK, who is a major participant in the high trapeze act in the Republican circus, trying to perform quadruple somersaults without a safety net. There is going to be an accident one day so for her own safety, she should have a net installed. The circus can be heard on radio, and seen on television, and college campuses. During an appearance at the University of Arizona, a pie was thrown at her for one of two reasons. Either the performance was bad, or she looked as if she needed it.

But let's give credit where it's due, she tries hard, and doesn't give up very easily.

1996: Hired by MSNBC as a legal correspondent. Fired in1997.

Bad performance?

1999-2000: Wanted to run for Congress from Connecticut on the Libertarian ticket, but the Party would not endorse her.

Bad performance?

2001: Contributing editor and syndicated columnist for National Review Online - Terminated after column was dropped.

Bad performance?

2005:- Arizona Daily Star dropped column after complaints from readers including conservatives.

Bad performance?

2006:- Augusta Chronicle dropped her column when the editor decided she was the "issue" rather than what she was writing about.

Bad performance?

2010:- A Canadian University cancelled a speech she was due to give.

Bad performance?

Engaged several times but never married "I wonder why".

Bad performances?

She reckons if Democrats had any brains they would be Republicans which is just another misguided statement. Even Republicans have brains, but Democrats are Democrats because they put theirs to good use. I think it's a real pity that brains are wasted on Republicans, because if they used their brains wisely, America would be a much better place, with much less crap polluting the atmosphere. Furthermore, if she regards herself as being so brainy, I suggest she opens some kind of learning institution, and have Palin, Brewer, and Angle as her first students.

Her desire to "bring down" President Clinton was so great that when Paula Jones decided on an out of court settlement, she quit the legal team. She suggested John Edwards was a faggot without actually calling him one, but later said she would never insult gays by suggesting they are like John Edwards, because that would be mean.

Finally, her outrageous comment,

"White people think everybody is inferior, and are perfectly charming about it"

Makes it so much easier to say that only one word can accurately describe her—"COULTERGEIST"

Laura Ingraham

SHE HAD AN EARLY START as a trouble maker. As a staff member of The Dartmouth Review, she implied that gay rights groups were "cheerleaders for latent campus sodomites" and is alleged to have secretly tape recorded the meetings and sent it to the members' parents. Paranoia set in and forced her to avoid eating at the local restaurant for fear of catching aids from homosexual waiters who might touch her utensils or spit in her food. I guess the homosexual waiters in other restaurants had defective hearing. The irony is, it turns out her brother is homosexual, and assuming they lived in the same house while growing up, he must have handled much more than her utensils.

Believe it or not, I wish no harm to anyone including Republicans, and for that reason I must congratulate her on her victory over cancer. She must realize however that she is like an "infectious cancer" in the Republican Party, and has therefore infected millions of people.

One evening I was flipping through the television channels, and stopped on CNN just in time to hear her say 'sleeveless doesn't always get what sleeveless wants', to rapturous applause from an "affected" audience. I realized she was taking a cheap shot at the First Lady while promoting her latest book "The Obama Diaries", which is supposed to be about a collection of diary entries made by President Obama. The following day I went to a book store and picked up a copy (no, I did not buy it). I read the introduction and my first reaction was, should I laugh or should I cry. I chose laughter and did a sharp, short, loud Chris Matthews "HA!" which got me suspicious stares from nearby customers.

She wants us to believe that on May 20, 2010 after spending forty-five minutes of sheer uninterrupted bliss having her pedicure, she went to the garage where her car was parked, saw an envelope laying on the hood of her car with the words,

"Property of the American People" scrawled on the front.

She goes on to say that as she lifted the envelope from the hood, a deep baritone voice called out,

"Just read it, you will know what to do with it"

His identity was obscured by the shadows, but she noticed that he was wearing high top sneakers.

She asked,

"Who are you? What is this about?"

But the man vanished. She then went into a bar and ordered a drink, found a little nook and ripped open the envelope. According to her, what she found took her breath away, and for almost two hours she sat transfixed, oblivious to the loud dance music booming over the speakers. The contents were (supposedly) excerpts from many of President Obama's hand written diaries, as well as Michele Obama and her mother, Marian Robinson and others. She then found herself aching for more after reading the last entry in the packet.

Wow! Did Laura create her own "aura" of mystery in that garage? Should Alfred Hitchcock call out from his grave and congratulate her? Was this another Republican on whom brains were wasted? Or was May 20, 2010 her day of infamy when she chose to launch another vicious smear attack on President Obama and his family?

I read a few more pages of her book, but stopped when I realized this was another example of a Republican Obama hater literally selling *good crap*. But, I also garnered one more thing from the book. This woman who had two fruitless engagements, was now fantasizing about a man who wears high top sneakers and has a deep baritone voice.

"Good hunting"

Back in 2006 on Election Day she encouraged listeners to jam the phone lines of a toll free Democratic Party service for reporting voting problems. Get a grip of yourself lady, your imagination is running wild and playing tricks on you, and may one day get you in some serious trouble. You started off at Dartmouth College, but if you continue in the same trend, even your law degree might not be able to save you from ending up in a place like Dartmouth Prison in England.

"Think it over"

Chapter 21

NEWT GINGRICH

THE NEWT was not man enough to put away his childish behavior when he helped to cause the shut down of the Federal Government in New York, because President Clinton made him sit at the back of Air Force One.

The Newt was ordered to pay $300,000.00 for the cost of an investigation into charges of ethics violations levied against him.

The Newt is alleged to have visited his wife in hospital while she was recovering from cancer to discuss divorce details.

The Newt tried to bring down Bill Clinton during the congressional investigation in the Monica Lewinsky incident.

The Newt was then discovered to be like a middle aged tiger hiding in the woods when his two timing hypocritical behavior was brought to light.

All of the above contributed to the Newt's political death. Now he's been reincarnated, and returned as a rabid brain damaged pit bull, his main purpose being to attack the President and infect the population. He's begun his attack by calling President Obama the most radical President in American history. He suggested,

> "Only if you understand Kenyan anti-colonial behavior can you begin to piece together his actions which are the most accurate predictive model of his behavior".

> "Health care reform", he says "is leading America to totalitarianism, authoritarianism, and the end of democracy".

The pit bull is one of the biggest hypocrites in American history, and only if you understand white racist mentality, can you begin to piece together his actions, which is the most accurate predictive model of his behavior. His "wealth care" for the rich will lead to total distrust of authority and the end of democracy in America's Republican Party.

Because there are so many weirdos now surfacing in the Republican Party, it was only natural that in time someone would eventually outdo the ridiculous "witch", and "lemon" moments presented by Christine O'Donnell and Sharon Angle, but no one believed it would come from the Newt. How can anyone, even his most loyal supporters buy his latest *crap* about his marital indiscretions being caused because of his great love for his country? Does that mean now that he's on the straight and narrow, his present wife is in no danger, until he starts loving his country again?

It's been suggested that he wants to have a crack at the Presidency in 2012 but carries so much baggage that it seems unlikely. If however he chooses to risk it, then I will reluctantly give him some advice.

"Be sure that your next female conquest goes by the name of Alice. Be sure to "See Alice" at least two hours before you give a speech, as this may help to cure your erect***, I'm sorry I meant "elective dysfunction".

"You really are a mess"

Chapter 22

Bill O'Reilly

THE REPUBLICAN NEWS NETWORK also known as Fox News Network is becoming a real joke, maybe because there are so many jokers working there. Kilmeade, a permanent fixture there claimed that all terrorists are Muslims. O'Reilly, (Billo) another permanent fixture went on ABC's program "The View", and thought it was OK to say Muslims were responsible for 9/11, and then later said he was not in the business of sugar coating harsh reality.

Not so long ago members of the KKK would get liquored up on a Saturday night then go out and hang or shoot innocent black men just for fun. Then on Sunday they would be in church with their families pretending to be Christians.

My question to you Mr. O'Reilly is this,

"If you were discussing this subject on The View would you be saying that white men or Christians perpetrated those crimes, or would you sugarcoat the harsh reality by saying the KKK did?"

I'm just asking.

I watched with great difficulty the so called interview he had with the President during the 2011 pre-Super Bowl program. It was painful to watch as he showed his disrespect for the President, by disrupting his answer to every question he asked. His intention was not to interview, but to intervene, interject, and interfere in an effort to agitate the President. He clearly forgot that he was dealing with someone far more talented than himself, and ended up showing the world the difference between a great Statesman like President Obama, and a sorry state of a man like Bill O'Reilly.

Yes really!

Chapter 23

PAT BUCHANAN

HE IS A DISASTER that started in the mid twentieth century, and has sadly rolled over into the twenty first with little change, and what is quite disturbing is that so many of these talk shows regularly have him on, giving credibility to his biased and sometimes racist opinions.

During the 2008 Presidential campaign he took pleasure in showing his disrespect, disregard, and disdain for then Senator Obama. He would refer to John McCain as Senator McCain, Sarah Palin as Governor Palin, Hillary Clinton as Senator Clinton, Joe Biden as Senator Biden, and Senator Barak Obama as "that community organizer from Chicago". That went on for months, with him having that look of satisfaction on his face every time he said it. No one intervened, until he appeared on MSNBC's program Morning Joe and used the same phrase, and Joe Scarborough to his credit simply said,

"He is also a United States Senator". I have not heard him use it since.

Based on his past and present statements and behavior it is easy to conclude that he is anti civil rights, by opposing so many civil rights laws and court decisions, anti semetic, by calling Capitol Hill the Israeli occupied territory. He called for the closing of the US Justice Department Office of Special Investigations which prosecuted Nazi war criminals, because in his opinion they were running down 70 year old camp guards.

His ridiculous anti-black question asking,

"Which would be easier to assimilate in Virginia? A million Zulus, or a million Englishmen?

He is anti-women (with the possible exception of Sarah Palin for whom he's probably got the hots and thinks she is winking directly at him).

When he said,

"Women are simply not endowed by nature with the same measures of single minded ambition, and the will to succeed in the fiercely competitive world of western capitalism. The real liberators of American women were not the feminist noise makers, but the automobile, the supermarket, the shopping center, the dishwasher, the washer dryer, and the freezer".

He is anti Martin Luther King, saying he would be outraged if Nixon visited King's widow on the first anniversary of his assassination because they deemed him a fraud, a demagogue, the devil incarnate, and one of the most divisive men in contemporary history.

On the other hand, it's easy to conclude that he was pro apartheid in South Africa, saying that the white minority rule of the black majority there was not inherently wrong, that Americans were collaborating in a United Nations conspiracy to ruin South Africa with sanctions.

Pro segregation by suggesting that multiculturalism was an assault on Anglo American heritage, and that the Negroes of the1940s and 50s of Washington had their public schools, restaurants, bars movie houses, and playgrounds, and we had ours.

Pro Hitler, by saying he was an individual of great courage, and a genius with extraordinary gifts. He thinks that thousands of Jews were not gassed to death by diesel exhaust at Treblenka, because in his opinion

"Diesel exhaust does not possess enough carbon monoxide to kill anybody".

I just wonder if he would be willing to take part in an experiment to prove his point.

Chapter 24

Family Ties

Ron Paul

DR. RON PAUL, Obstetrician. He chose a great profession in which he is able to help with the birth of children. The pity is in the way he chooses to treat some of them when they grow up.

So let me ask these questions.

"Did President Nixon know about Watergate?"

"Did President Bush know that Sadaam Hussein had nothing to do with 9/11?"

"Did Dick Cheney know about the outing of Valerie Plame?"

Was Ron Paul responsible for statements published in his newsletter some of which read?

"Boy it sure burns me to have a National Holiday for that pro-communist philanderer M.L.K. I voted against this outrage time and time again as a Congressman".

"What an infamy that Ronald Reagan approved it. We can thank him for our annual hate whitey day"

"I've urged every one in my family to learn how to use a gun in self defense for the animals are coming".

Did he draw his conclusion from a 1992 study produced by the Center of Incarceration and Alternatives that "95%of black males are semi criminals, or fully criminals"? Did he suggest that polls show only 5% of blacks have sensible political opinions?

Based on the above, and the many other controversial statements he has made, do you believe Ron Paul is a racist?

You decide.

Rand Paul

LIKE FATHER, LIKE SON. As the saying goes, "The chip never falls far from the block". He is also in the medical field as an ophthalmologist, but is now behaving more like a segregationist. This newly elected Tea Party Senator said, had he been a Senator in the sixties he would have questioned the constitutionality of the Civil Rights Act, which prohibits private businesses who provide public accommodation from discriminating on the basis of race, religion, or national origin, against their customers, because it infringes upon constitutional freedom.

He says he does not like the idea of the Feds determining who a business should serve, then in the same breath says he abhors racism. Tell that to a dead donkey, and it would get up and kick the crap out of him, leaving him nothing else to sell. Somehow all the blame can not be laid on him, because of the environment in which he was brought up. He must have been influenced by those racist remarks made by his father, but he is not a child any more, and should know better. Apparently he has decided to follow in father's footsteps.

Chapter 25

New Kids on the Block

(Christie & Brewer)
Chris Christie

NEW JERSEY'S LATEST Governor, admired and loved by all Republicans for the time being that is. Did he really use his power as attorney general to tarnish Democrats? Did he really bend the rules to his advantage, and made taxpayers pay for his suites at the Four Seasons hotel? Did he really kill the new rail tunnel project to be built under the Hudson River, because the State could not afford it or, did he have an ulterior motive?

I'm sure he knows that billions of dollars are being spent on infra-structure in Iraq and Afghanistan, without any questions asked about where the money is coming from. I'm also sure he knows that killing the tunnel project would make New Jersey residents the "Biggest Losers". What I didn't realize, until I saw him on television, and he removed his jacket is that he was seeking allies in his constituents.

Because he is a prime candidate for television's reality show "Biggest Loser"

Go for it.

Jan Brewer

IT IS NO LONGER a mystery why the Republican Party of the Abraham Lincoln era has sunk to its current new low. The simple answer is that it's now over-run by a large number of cranks, like the one I am about describe. The Governor of Arizona obviously had no control over her given name, "Drinkwine", but based on her behavior she seems to have been practicing too much of what her name suggests. She had full control over her new name, but chose it anyway, maybe because she wanted to brew her own brand of wine. That would easily account for her hallucinatory claims of headless corpses in the desert and apparent memory loss in an interview. She should try Hannity who might be willing to give her the viewing treatment only, where looks, not words matter. In her case did I really suggest looks?

If she were sober when she passed budget cuts that stopped transplant funding that was previously promised to Arizonians, causing some of them to die, could that be a case of criminal insanity on her part? If the answer is Yes, then she should get the same sentence as her son who was charged with a similar offence.

Chapter 26

THE HOUSE CONTROLLERS

(Boehner & Cantor)
John Boehner

FINALLY HIS AMBITION has been realized. Before he even got sworn in he said this is not a time to compromise, and called the vote for middle class tax cuts "chicken shit". He is wrong in this case, but as a Republican he should be an expert on the excrement of chickens, and all the other animals, as that is what Republicans dress up and sell to their supporters with such great success. One would have thought that with eleven siblings, and knowing what poverty is all about, he would be the first to welcome an extension of unemployment benefits for the unemployed, and this is when he should be saying "Hell No to tax cuts for millionaires".

Oh no, not him. The new found highlife has stunted his memory, and one can guess from this and past behavior just what kind of a speaker he is going to be.

In his November 2010 victory speech his eyes welled-up as he has done on several previous occasions. He spoke with a lot of emotion about spending his whole life chasing the American dream, and got sympathetic cheers from his supporters.

He refused an invitation from the President to attend a memorial service in Tucson, Arizona honoring the victims of the senseless act of violence that occurred there, his excuse being that he had a previous engagement. I watched the President's speech in its entirety, and thought that if John Boehner were there, there were so many moments during the speech when he would have genuine reasons to tear up, but instead he chose the wine and laughter of a fund raising function.

"There is a time to laugh, and a time to cry, Sir. The day of the memorial service was definitely not a time to laugh."

No one knows for sure what kind of a leader he will be, only time will tell, but in my opinion he is off to a poor start. I was helped with this conclusion because his campaign in 2010 was all about "where are the jobs?" Yet he has gone on TV, stared at the cameras, bright-eyed and tear-free, and lied about the number of new jobs the President added to the Federal workforce, and then said,

"If his (Republican) policies caused some of them to lose their jobs" then, *"SO BE IT!"*

Coming from him it is difficult to ignore the first three letters in the phrase "S.O.B". We are all aware of his tear-shedding problem, but his emphasis should be on "JOB" rather than "S.O.B"

He said,

"Hell No!" to health-care for millions,

"So be it!" to Americans losing their jobs, and

"Read my lips! We are going to cut spending" (as long as it's not his state)

So what's next? Will it be?

"Make my day!", because now that I am Speaker of the House

"Frankly, I don't give a damn"?

He says he agrees that the President was born in Hawaii, but is afraid to tell his supporters so, because they may be offended by the truth. I watched as he received the gavel from Nancy Pelosi his predecessor, and wondered why she did not hand him a box of tissues as well. After all she was introducing the new "Weeper" of the House.

Eric Cantor

THE HOUSE MAJORITY LEADER who always appears to be standing beside, and sometimes behind John Boehner with that ridiculous grin on his face. It is difficult to tell whether he is laughing with him or at him. So now the Republicans have a Weeper, and a Grinner in the House.

Lately, the word "we" seems to have taken on a new political significance. This became quite clear in the Tea Partiers slogan, "we want our country back", and the Grinners comments "if we want America to be what we want America to be". Obviously "we" means Tea Partiers and Republicans, (one and the same) because they believe that America belongs to them only. The Grinner's way of achieving his goal is to abolish Social Security and Medicare. Yet he will sell it in such a way, that even the Senior Citizens that he wants to deprive of their entitled benefits from a program to which they have contributed all their working lives, will still vote for him.

He had no problem with spending during the Bush Administration, but has a problem with it under the Obama Administration, even when it was the only way to stop America's financial decline.

He had no problem defending John Barton's apology to BP in the wake of the oil disaster that threatened to destroy the Gulf region.

But he had a problem giving an opinion on Ron Paul's criticism of the Civil Rights Act.

He had a problem deciding whether he was for or against Arizona's controversial Immigration Bill.

He had a problem releasing details of threatening emails he claimed to have received.

He has a problem alright, because after taking away benefits from the poor, he wants them to do more with less. After giving more to the rich with huge tax breaks, they will do less with more. He either **can't-or,** he can do the right thing, but he will canter along with his colleagues, as they continue in their effort to deceive the people in believing that they want to provide jobs even when their behavior suggests otherwise.

Chapter 27

THE EX's
(HUCKABEE, ROMNEY & GUILLIANI)

Mike Huckabee

I FIRST BECAME AWARE of the ex-governor of Arkansas in 2008 when he began his campaign for the Republican Presidential nomination, and my first impression after hearing him for the first time, was how refreshing for a Republican. Barack Obama became the Democratic front runner, and then out of Huckabee's mouth came,

"That was Barack Obama, he just tripped off a chair. He is getting ready to speak. Somebody aimed a gun at him, and he dove for the floor"

Those were his words. He may have apologized for this sick joke, which got him a few laughs, but many true words have been spoken in jest, and although many may have those thoughts, he is the only politician who has actually have some one pointing a gun at the now President. Naturally I started to see him in a different light, which got dimmer and dimmer as time went by.

I saw him in an interview with CBS, Katie Couric, who has the ability to get the worst out of people by asking simple questions. She asked him what he would he have done differently had he been in the President's place, and instead of answering the question, he mumbled on about families tightening their belts in times of hardship (at least he didn't follow the old Republican line of "cut taxes"). She asked him if he would have liked to have seen General Motors collapse. Instead of answering the question he mentioned driving GM cars for over thirty years. Like all the others he had no answers for solving America's problems, but is full of criticism.

The lights dimmed to a mere glimmer after the radio appearance, where he said that he would like to know more about Barack Obama but what he knew was troubling enough. Does that positive statement sound like miss-speaking? He continued by saying that the President grew up in Kenya with his father and grandfather which made his view of the British different from the average American.

He suggested that the President had a hostile attitude to Britain, and that his removal of Winston Churchill's bust from the White House was an insult to the British, conveniently forgetting to mention that he replaced it with a bust of President Abraham Lincoln. Although the President has been a model American citizen, (more so than many of his Republican critics), many top Republicans including Huckabee have done everything in their power to brand him as un-American. My question to Mr. Huckabee and all the others would be this. Based on this bust incident, who would you say is more American, the President who placed the bust of a great British Prime Minister in the White House, or the President who removed it and replaced it with the bust of a great American President?

I for one do not believe it was a slip of the tongue, but a deliberate bold-faced attempt to pander to the far right base in an effort to capture their votes should he decide to run for

President. These are the low down tactics that Republicans now use, throw the lies out there and sometimes apologize later, because once it out there, someone will always buy their *Good Crap*.

He says that music is his passion, and if he could get a permanent gig, he would put tattoos all over his body, and grow his hair down to his rear end. What a sight that would be.

It's not too late, just start your own band, and since you say Sarah Palin is the Rock star of your party, she may be the first to join up.

All is not lost for Mr Huckabee, because he is a well paid employee of the Fox News Network establishment, and may be considering another crack at the Republican Presidential nomination. If he wins, we would know what to expect from him. Our borders would instantly be secured, because he would send Chuck Norris to secure them. The leaders of North Korea and Iran would no longer present a threat to the USA, because he would send Chuck Norris to deal with them. This man Norris is so powerful that he pushes the earth down when he does press-ups, and since he is in favor of secession for Texas, he will definitely be able to push Texas off the North American continent to make it a separate country. I advise Norris to be very careful though, because while he is busy doing all this, "The Dragon May Return".

I should not be disappointed in the behavior of any Republican, because they are nearly all alike, but somehow I am disappointed in Huckabee, because as an ordained minister, he ought to be a man of God. But politics have changed him. I think he believes that by becoming President, it will make him a "God of men".

Mitt Romney

THIS EX-MASSACHUSETTS Governor is a front runner for the Republican Presidential nomination, and like his colleagues thinks he has the answers to all of America's problems. He has managed to convince himself and some supporters that his success as a businessman is the qualification needed to make him a great President. He must have forgotten that as a businessman, he made millions by taking over companies and getting rid of workers, therefore contributing to rising unemployment.

The problem is, does America want a wishy-washy character who will say anything , true or false to get votes, to be their President? He said he saw his father march with MLK, when he did not.

If he likened the threat of same sex marriage to the menace of Islamist terrorists, as President, would he deal with both issues in the same way?

How could a potential President equate the support of his sons for him, with that of the men and women in the armed forces who put themselves in harms way in defending their Country?

Will this multi millionaire be willing to risk another forty million dollars of his own money to go to Washington, the place they all hate so much? Workers in the car and affiliated industries, just remember you would now be among the unemployed if Romney had his way, because he said he would have voted against the bailout of Chrysler and General Motors.

Welcome to the race Mr. Romney, you are a sure fire winner.

Rudy Giuliani

"A NOUN, A VERB, AND 9/11 epitomizes this former New York City Mayor, and 2008 Republican Presidential candidate.

A lot could be said about this man, but I would be doing Vice-President Joe Biden a disservice if I added anything to the most telling seven word description of any one in the 2008 Presidential campaign.

Maybe I could say no nouns or verbs in 2012. Enough said.

Chapter 28
THE TWO MASCOTS
(BROWN & WALKER)

Scott Brown

ONE OF THE MORE moderate Republicans, Scott Brown against all odds overcame childhood abuse and grew up to be a successful individual, and against all odds he managed to replace Ted Kennedy as Senator of Massachusetts.

I read the interview he had with Sean Hannity, and was impressed by the way he resisted Hannity's persistent pressure on him to demonize President Obama.

Maybe against all odds, he will continue to be his own man.

Scott Walker

The people of the State of Wisconsin, blinded by the lies of the Republican propaganda machine, elected Scott Walker to be their Governor. Like the people of many other states, the people of Wisconsin are beginning to regret their actions. They made their beds and now have to lay in them, and will have to do so until they have the opportunity to remake them. They now realize that he does not represent them, but himself and his wealthy bosses. His behavior has caused so much disruption in his State and others, that it leaves me to wonder,

Is he trying to rob people of collective bargaining in order to collect the bargain of a good time in California that he was promised, especially if it included drinks with a couple of "Kochs" as chasers.

"Shame on You"

Chapter 29

KARL ROVE

THIS IS THE REPUBLICAN'S MR. FIX-IT, and Escape Artist. The Bush Administration's right hand man. He can fix anything and always has an escape plan.

He has been said to have been involved in Administration energy policy meetings, while at the same time holding stock in energy companies including Enron, but escaped conflict of interest charges.

He has been alleged to have caused the dismissal of U.S Attorneys, but he escaped the allegations.

He has been accused of email scandals, but escaped the scandals.

He has been accused of improper political influence over government decision making, but escaped the accusations.

He was Senior Advisor to President Bush, but escaped from the Bush Administration in August, 2007.

He is said to have criticized the Liberals response to 9/11

by implying that Liberals saw the savagery of the 9/11 attacks, but wanted to prepare indictments, and offer therapy and understanding for our attackers. He escaped without apologizing, and with a small slap on the wrist by 9/11 families who asked him to stop trying to reap political gain from the tragic misfortune of others.

He has been accused of ties to the "Swift Boat Veterans for Truth" television advertisements that criticized John Kerry's Vietnam military service, but escaped.

He has been accused of planting fake anti-Bush documents with CBS News in an effort to deflect attention from Bush's service record during the Vietnam War, but escaped when no supporting evidence was produced.

He has been accused of leaking the identity of Valerie Plame, a CIA employee, but escaped because no charges were filed against him.

He sure would give Harry Houdini a very good run for his money, but as the saying goes,

"If you take the same bucket to the well every day, one day the bottom is going to fall out"

"Take heed, there may be a hole in your bucket dear Karl".

Chapter 30

MITCH McCONNELL

THE NUMBER ONE Republican Senator whose job is not to serve the people who elected him, or Americans in general, but by his own words to make President Obama a one term President.

That statement will go down very well with some, if not all of his supporters, but the majority of Americans will now see him in a different light. Maybe his new job description is based on the fact that he did not get Harry Reid's job.

Nevertheless, he has shown the American people what the main objective of the Republican Party is, and it definitely has nothing to do with jobs.

"America, his fate is in your hands", (or is it "arms" according to the Ernor)

Chapter 31

THE FRINGE ELEMENT

THERE ARE MANY MORE REPUBLICANS out there that deserve a mention, some of whom I am not even aware.

There is Michael Savage who is a credit to his name.

There is Jim DeMint the Tea Party champion, and the only mint to leaves a bad taste in the mouth.

There is Rick Santorum who needs his head examined if he thinks President Obama's race should influence his views on abortion. Insert two "I's" in the appropriate places in his surname to find the place he needs to be.

There is Tim Pawlenty who publicly admits he is suffering from bedroom starvation.

There is Sharon Angle who wanted to take Harry Reid "OUT"

There is Christine O'Donnell who thinks that American mice are running around with fully functioning human brains.

There is Heidi Harris whose brain should give her mouth a speeding ticket.

There is Joe Watkins the Pastor, but really a Minister of His Own Affairs.

There is Dick Morris who failed in his bid to be a crystal ball.

There is Amy Holmes who says she loves photo shoots, and will more than likely continue to shoot crap as long as it gets her on television.

There is Michelle Malkin who will definitely stay away from balls especially if they are hard, and thrown by Chris Matthews.

There is Haley Barbour who after 63 years has decided that the Mississippi of his teenage years was a warm and peaceful place.

There is Paul Brown who pacified his supporters when one of them asked him "Who is going to shoot Obama"?

There is Paul Ryan who wants to destroy Social Security and Medicare so he can save them later.

There is Pat Robertson who thinks he gets messages directly from God, and believes the earthquake that devastated Port au Prince, Haiti is a blessing in disguise because of a pact made with the devil.

There is Donald Trump. Because of the decline in real estate this Republican apprentice has decided to go slumming by trying to outsell his colleagues in the thriving "*good crap*" market.

Yes, there are many more, but most of the main offenders have been dealt with.

Chapter 32

MR. PRESIDENT

PRESIDENT BARACK OBAMA, let me use this opportunity to offer belated congratulations on your successful and history making Presidential campaign, which made you the first African American President of these United States. For some reason your success reminds me of a young King Solomon who was given wisdom, knowledge, and understanding after he became King. You however Mr. President, was fortunate enough to be given wisdom, knowledge, and understanding before you became President. All three gifts were necessary for you to achieve your goal. You showed remarkable wisdom in dealing with the hateful rhetoric thrown at you throughout the campaign, and which has continued ever since then. You gained a vast amount of knowledge through your academic achievements, and your spell as a Community Organizer gave you first hand understanding of things that past Presidents did not understand.

Since becoming President you have been wrongfully blamed for many of the disasters you inherited. Two years later the people spoke with their votes in the 2010 election, and Republicans gained many seats in the House, which they now control, and some in the Senate which has drastically reduced the Democratic majority. The Republicans joyfully claim that their success is a result of the people's rejection of your policies. "Wrong". Nothing could be further from the truth, because most of the voters did not even hear of your policies and their successful results, simply because they were drowned by the deafening drum beat of lies and distorted sales pitch from the Republicans. Over the years they have perfected the art of lying, and much more successful at lying than Democrats are at telling the truth.

The Japanese attack on Pearl Harbor took place in 1941, and for the next sixty years there were no significant attacks on American soil by foreign sources, until the 9/11 attack on the World Trade Center in 2001 under the George Bush administration. Yet all we hear from Republicans is that President Bush kept us safe for eight years.

"SOLD"

You have achieved more than any other president in your first two years. Yet all we hear from republicans is Obama has done nothing.

"SOLD"

You signed a health care bill into law, which will give coverage to millions of uninsured Americans. Yet all we hear from Republicans is "government take-over, let's repeal it".

"SOLD"

The bill helps lower the cost of prescriptions for senior citizens. Yet all we hear from Republicans is "death panels".

"SOLD"

It allows children to stay on their parent's insurance policies until age 26. Yet all we hear from Republicans is "Obama care".

"SOLD"

You saved the country from sinking into a depression. Yet all we hear from Republicans is "government is too big".

"SOLD"

You stopped the Collapse of the motor car industry. Yet all we hear from Republicans is too much government intervention.

"SOLD"

You have created thousands of jobs, and saved millions of people from loosing their jobs. Yet all we hear from Republicans, "he has not created any jobs".

"SOLD"

Then, there are the vicious personal attacks.

"You are the most corrupt president in history"

"SOLD"

"You are an illegal alien, because you were not born in America"

"SOLD"

"You are a Muslim, the anti Christ, and a communist"

"SOLD"

"You would be spending $200,000,000 per day on your proposed 2010 November trip to India, with 34 navy ships diverted for your protection"

"SOLD"

On top of all this, Mitch McConnell has said that his Party's main priority is to make you a one term President, while John Boehner said this is not a time to compromise, and that he rejects the word compromise. Theirs are the voices of the Republican Party, and have been plotting your failure from day one. Being the gentleman that you are, you may not openly admit it, but the whole world knows that your race plays a big part in the disgraceful way the Republicans have been treating you, because no other President, no matter how disliked by them, has ever been disrespected in this way.

In 2008 after your historical victory, you sat down with the Republicans and asked them to join you in helping to move the country forward, but they opposed everything you placed on the table, because their objective was your failure. And their motto, to just say "No" to everything, and you would fail. The 2010 election has signaled the arrival of a new bunch of Tea Partiers, all suffering from the AIDS (acquired immune disruptive syndrome) virus, which has spread through the Party like an uncontrollable forest fire. They have joined with all the other "repealicans" in asking you to compromise, their interpretation of compromise being their way, or the highway. I don't think so, because in a compromise, there should be mutual concessions from both Parties, give a little, and get a little. They want to give nothing, and get everything.

You have asked for their help, but it has not been given. You have knocked on their doors, but they have not opened, instead they have added more locks. You have been slapped on both cheeks, and you don't have a third to turn. You have completely exhausted the idea that if at first you don't succeed, you should try, try, and try again. It is time to take a stand. Please do not abandon your principles to this bunch of crazies and give in to everything they want. That would not be compromise, but compromised capitulation on your part, something your supporters would not want. Your supporters just want you to stick to your principles, and turn your loud speakers to their maximum so that every one can hear you, know that Barack Obama is still the President of these United States and will continue to do the job he promised to do.

The reality is, as you know Mr. President, there are flat surfaces on the earth, but the earth is round, and one placed beside another one is eleven, but one plus one is two. So, stick to the facts and you cannot go wrong. It is better to fail attempting to do what is right, than to succeed in implementing the wrong ideas of the Republican haters.

Over the years, all the black folks who are now regarded as great Americans faced violent and sometimes deadly resistance on their journey to greatness. Based on your achievements Mr. President, you have already acquired the status of great American, and just like those before you, the resistance will continue, but you will survive because, with the exception of America's racist minority, the majority of whom are Republicans, you are loved by all other Americans, and revered by the citizens of countries all over the world, who wished they had a leader like you. But it's a well known fact that people don't always appreciate what they have until they lose it. Hopefully most Americans will not fall into that category, and we will enjoy your leadership until 2016.

Of course the people were frustrated by the state of the economy, and sky-high unemployment, and showed it with their votes. But even then they were smart enough to reject some of those who insisted women who got pregnant through incestuous rape, should be forced to have children, those who wanted to end unemployment benefits, and those who claimed to have dabbled in witchcraft.

The year 2012 will soon be upon us, and your policies will be more defined and heard. The dust of 2010 will have settled, the dark clouds will have disappeared and people will be able to see more clearly. They will speak again in November of 2012, but in larger numbers and louder voices and once again it will be overwhelmingly on your behalf. Remember that you still have millions of supporters who want you to stay in the driver's seat and successfully lead America back to its rightful place on top of the world.

Your historical achievement has brought joy to many Americans, and given time I am quite sure that you will satisfy all of their "Great Expectations".

They are with you all the way because they know **you can**.

Chapter 33

The First Lady

YOU HAVE BEEN A REVELATION, a true example of someone that African American women and women in general should try to emulate.

I have noticed that the Ernor uses every opportunity she gets to throw a few jabs at you, by saying things like,

"You are un-American"

This is probably an effort to drag you into a dog fight, but I know you will not sink to that level. The fact is you are the First Lady, and you will not get into a war of words. You are not a hockey mom or a grizzly mom with daughters running awry, but just a regular loving mother with two wonderful daughters being brought up in a stable environment.

You don't need to legitimize the new female Republican phrase "man up" by clubbing fish to death, or shooting harmless animals in an effort to prove your equality to men, because you possess such exceptional qualities. You don't have to use ropes to try and climb insignificant hills, because with your parents' inspiration and your dedication, you have reached the top of the significant mountain that Martin Luther King spoke about. You don't have to look at the lay of the land to see if there is a Democrat out there that is suitable to run for President, because you are married to the Democratic President of the United States of America.

You are doing what you can to address the problem of child obesity, while the Ernor tries to undo your work by stuffing children with cookies.

So let's see, you are America's First Lady, you are not into mud-slinging, you were instrumental in getting the "Healthy, Hunger-Free Kids Bill" passed in an effort to keep American children healthy. You are a loving parent, wife, daughter, sister, and friend. And you love your country. If that is un-American, then congratulations are in order because there are millions of Americans who would like their children to grow up and be just as "un-American" as you.

However I have one suggestion. If anyone should ever again publicly ask you,

"What do you think of Sarah Palin?"

You need two words only,

"I don't".

Chapter 34

A Message to African Americans

THROUGHOUT HISTORY, and in countries all over the world, black people have excelled in every walk of life, sometimes under extraordinarily terrible conditions, and opposition. However, they refused to give up and persevered in their endeavors, making the seemingly impossible become possible. On whom will history shine its brightest light? Will it be the achievers or their offenders?

Will it be "Nanny" the Ghanian born queen of the Windward Maroons of Jamaica, who fled to the hills with her people to avoid enslavement by the British, and led them spiritually culturally and militarily until they got their freedom, or the British army that tried to impose the brutality of slavery upon them?

Will it be Booker T Washington who dedicated his life to having the necessary schools built to help blacks achieve a good education, knowing that was the best way for them to have a better future, or the two racists, James K Vardman soon to be governor of Mississippi, and Benjamin Tillman, Senator of South Carolina who made those disgusting obscene comments when President Roosevelt invited Washington to the White House?

Vardman once said,

"The White House is so saturated with the smell of nigger, that the rats have taken refuge in the stables".

Tillman commented,

"The action of President Roosevelt in entertaining that nigger necessitates the killing of one thousand niggers in the south before they will learn their place again"

Will it be Marcus Garvey of Jamaica who formed the Universal Negro Improvement Association, in an effort to unite black people allover the world ,or assistant District Attorney Edwin P Kilroe who is alleged to have sent George Tyler to kill Garvey?.

Will it be Toussaint L'Ouverture who led his country Haiti to independence despite facing grave danger and opposition, or Napoleon who requested a meeting with him, but betrayed him and had him imprisoned in a mountain dungeon where he eventually died of neglect and starvation?

Will it be Martin Luther King the great civil rights advocate who was beaten, spat on, imprisoned, and finally murdered all because he dared to want equal rights for blacks, or J Edgar Hoover who branded King a communist and abused his position as head of the FBI to try and stop him by any means necessary?

Will it be Nelson Mandela who was imprisoned for most of his adult life, because he fought to have his people treated as human beings but was eventually released and made President of South Africa?, or John Vorster, the Leader of South Africa's oppressive government, who eventually had to resign because of a political scandal?

Will it be Jesse Owens who suffered intense racism at home

but represented his country in the 1936 olympics, where he won four gold medals in track and field events, a record that lasted for decades before it was equaled by another African American, Carl Lewis, or Adolf Hitler who physically showed his annoyance at Owens' success, and later told Albert Speer, that Owens was a descendant of primitive people of the jungle with stronger physiques than those of civilized whites, and hence should be excluded from future games?

Will it be Pele the world's greatest footballer of all time who first represented his country Brazil in the world cup at the tender age of seventeen, or the English football club manager who said that as long as he was the manager, no blacks would be allowed to play on his team even if his name were Pele?

Will it be Marian Anderson the celebrated black contralto who faced so much racism especially during her early years , but was honored in January 2005 with a commemorative postage stamp, or the woman at the admissions counter of the all white Philadelphia Music Academy who said "we don't take blacks" when Marian made her application to attend?

Will it be Harriet Tubman the slave who ran away when the whippings and gross living conditions became too much to bear, and helped guide many other slaves to freedom, and helped newly freed slaves find work, or the various slave masters who relentlessly whipped her?

Will it be Jackie Robinson who in 1947 became the First African American to play in major league baseball, but had to deal with racial taunts from the crowd and some team mates who threatened to "sit out" rather than play with him, or the commander of the army's 758th battalion (of which Robinson was a member), who consented to charge him with offences including drunkenness even though he was a teetotaler?

Will it be Muhammad Ali the greatest boxer of all time, who was threatened with imprisonment and stripped of his boxing license basically because he became a Muslim, or the members of the boxing association who suspended his license?

Will it be Oprah Winfrey one of the most admired and respected women in the world, whose unequalled generosity has changed the lives of thousands around the globe for the better, and Now has Won with OWN, or Rush Limbaugh who lost the right to own a football club he so badly wanted, and whose daily ranting and ravings include suggestions that Oprah is wealthy and successful because she is black, and not because she is gifted, and talented?

Will it be Barack Obama, who defied overwhelming odds to become America's first African American President, or John McCain who embarrassed himself, his Party, his Country, and the World, when he Chose Sarah Palin as his running mate in his 2008 Presidential bid, which thankfully was unsuccessful, and did not deprive history of one of its greatest moments?

Many of these questions have already been answered, and the answers to the rest are so obvious.

It is a great feeling to be able to sing the praises of some of the world's great black people, past and present, but sadly there are times when I agree with the saying that "the black man's worst enemy is himself", especially here in America.

There is the story of a black man who opened a store, and on his first day of business, a friend came in and asked for credit claiming he had no money. The owner explained to him that this was his first day and he could not yet start giving credit to anyone. His friend got mad and stormed out of the shop, walked to the white-owned shop a block away and paid cash for the goods he wanted. That is the warped mentality of some black folks.

When Senator Obama declared his intention to seek the Democratic Presidential nomination an African American said to me,

"Obama will have to prove himself to me if he wants my vote".

"Did you vote for Bill Clinton"? I asked.

"Yes" he replied

"And did he have to prove himself to you to get your vote"?

"Well", was his answer.

I am a big fan of the Clintons, because I think Bill Clinton was a great President, and his wife Hillary Clinton, an exceptional former First Lady, who went on to become a very good, well respected Senator. So I had no problem with anyone who chose to support Senator Clinton in her bid for the Democratic Presidential nomination, but what really shocked me was the reason one prominent African American gave for supporting Senator Clinton instead of Senator Obama. He once was the Guest Speaker at a function celebrating Jamaica's Independence, and spoke of the times in the fifties when he would visit Jamaica with Dr. King, and was really thrilled to see Jamaicans running things themselves. He wished the same thing for African Americans here in the United States and worked very hard with others to achieve that goal.

Now fifty years later here comes a brilliant, dynamic, capable young man in Barack Obama, and his reason for not supporting him was that "he should wait his turn". That was such a disappointing statement coming from someone for whom I had such great admiration and respect.

It is really sad to hear an African American especially a mature man say he is worried when he is getting on a plane and see people dressed in garb that identifies them first and foremost as Muslims. Yet he never says he fears people dressed in garb that may identify them as a Timothy McVeigh, or a Charles Manson, or a Jarod Loughner. How can anyone identify such people should be the question asked?

The answer is the same way African Americans are identified and sometimes shunned, by the color they permanently wear. Not so long ago, in the sixties to be more precise, a young black kid In London, England mugged an English woman and ran off with her purse, and soon after, all young black men in England were branded as muggers. White women especially the older ones were afraid if it even appeared they were being approached by black men. It so happened that not long after the mugging incident, an elderly English woman was trying to cross a busy street, and a young black man approached her in an effort to help her across the street, but he was wearing the wrong color, so the woman screamed and started hitting the young man with her walking stick. Only then did the white folks who did not help her when she really needed help, decided to help. I am sure that in the past, and even now here in America some Caucasians are still afraid when they are approached by people dressed in a different color than theirs, but you Sir, an African American are scared of people dressed like Muslims.

I saw a young black woman publicly shed tears almost to the point of hysteria when Senator Obama finally beat Senator Clinton. I saw a young black man at a Town Hall meeting stand up and begged Senator McCain to sock it to Senator Obama. I watched as another black woman with the name of Hart prove that her heart was in the wrong place, when she said she was tired of defending the President, and literally blamed him for her middle class demise. That was such a shame just to gain her moment of television fame. A black student asked the President why he should vote for him again when he did not fulfill the promise of change he made.

"Jesus wept. What is wrong with these people"?

"Have they lost their senses? Can't they see what's going on"?

Shouldn't this be the time to say?

"Mr. President we can see what you are up against with Republicans doing every thing in their power to make you fail, not to mention the racist outbursts thrown in your direction".

"But don't worry, Sir, we've got your back".

Cheney and his gang started an unnecessary war in Iraq, which took the lives of thousands of Americans, and Iraqis, maimed tens of thousands, at a cost of hundreds of billions of dollars to this country, yet people like Ron Christie and other "black Obama haters" defend that gang daily without ever saying they are tired of defending them. Something is definitely wrong with that picture, and President Obama does not deserve the type of negative criticism he gets from some of these selfish, fickle-minded black people, whose only interest is in personal gain.

No other President in the history of the United States, from George Washington to George Bush has ever inherited the disaster that this President inherited. Just take a few minutes and think about it. Two costly wars with no end in sight, the worst recession in living memory for most people, a deficit of hundreds of billions of dollars, the loss of seven hundred and fifty thousand jobs each month, and after less than two years he was expected to fix it all.

I know some people also expected him to walk on water or to turn water into wine. Well he did not, but at least give him some credit for the near miracles he did perform, like health care and financial reform. Please be reminded that he is not our Savior. Our Savior was betrayed and crucified over 2000 years ago to save mankind. The chief priests and elders persuaded the people to vote to save Barrabas rather than Jesus. I am by no means comparing President Obama with Jesus, but he is basically in a similar situation. The chief priests and elders of the Republican Party are trying to persuade people to choose between either the President and the Democrat Party that is trying to move the country forward, or "the mamma grizzlies, witches, chicken ladies, lemon ladies, madams, civil rights rejecters, minimum wage objectors, social security privateers, medicare, and medicaid dismantlers, minimum wage destroyers, and all the other nut cases that keep crawling out of the Republican woodwork.

Sadly these are the titles of some of the candidates representing the Republican Party which is at a new low, never been reached before in their long and controversial history. The President is only human, and is doing the best he can under the current circumstances, with the Republicans doing every thing they can to make him fail. Democrats call them the Party of "No".

Sarah Palin the new face of their Party confirmed it with much stronger language,

"We are the Party of Hell No!" she says, and gets paid thousands of dollars for those and other outrageous remarks.

When I listen to some of the radio programs, I hear African Americans complaining that Obama is President because of their vote and that he's done so much for Mexicans and Jews and nothing for them. What a load of baloney. Sure the black vote helped him to become President, but if every black person in the country voted for him and no whites or Mexicans did, he would not be President today.

So what has he done differently for Jewish or Mexican Americans who are citizens of this country that he has not done for African American citizens? As far as I know he hasn't treated one minority differently from the other. He is trying to address the illegal immigration problem where the majority of illegals are Mexicans, but don't forget there are illegal African and West Indian immigrants also. Is that what is meant by helping the Mexicans?

Israel has always been an ally of the United States, and he is also trying to address the Israel/Palestine problem. Is that what is meant by helping the Jews?

This President though black, did not promise to be President of "Black America", but of "All America", so stop belly-aching and give the man a chance and the time to do his job. None of the previous 43 Presidents were infallible or indispensable, they all made mistakes, and when their term was up or they got voted out, they were replaced. The same applies to President Obama, but while he is in office, for heaven's sake, give him the opportunity to make good on his promises and the respect he deserves.

Blacks have been surviving in America ever since they were stolen from Africa, and brought here. They were brought here against their will and they survived. They were classed as part human, and they survived. They were sold into slavery and they survived. They were brutally beaten and they survived. They were not allowed to learn to read and write, and they survived. They were not allowed to own land, and they survived. They were not allowed to vote, and they survived. They went overseas to fight for their country only to return home to be treated like second class citizens, and they survived.

Today, some have finally achieved the "American Dream", and have now started to live, but many are still only surviving, and it's up to them to take the necessary steps to turn things around.

Stop thinking of the President as a Savior, and start doing some of the things he has suggested. Parents, be there for your children. Invest more time in their education, ensuring they are aware of their history because they are America's future. Do what you can to stop black on black crime and crime in general.

People who commit crimes should be punished, but the punishment should fit the crime. Allowing two black women to serve 16 years in prison for an $11.00 robbery is completely out of order, and the Judge who imposed that sentence should be sent to prison for 16 years. The prisons are full of innocent blacks and other minorities. This brings to mind the fact that one white thief has "Made-off" with more money than the total amount stolen by all the worlds black thieves over the same period of time, and probably over all time.

Those who can, should give back to their communities, and above all, invest strongly in your spiritual growth. You should go to church to worship God and sing his praises, not to display "bling" and fancy clothes. During Jesus' time, the chariot was probably the equivalent to today's Rolls Royce, but Jesus went into Jerusalem on Palm Sunday, on the then lowest form of transportation, a donkey which he did not even own.

Be wary of those mega churches, because they are exactly what their names suggest. Mega buildings, mega congregation, mega dollars in mega bank accounts, and yes mega egos that sometimes cause mega problems. I am not suggesting all the ministers of these mega churches are con artists, but so many have fallen from grace through financial and sexual scandals, that questions have to be asked and hopefully answered. It does not matter whether they are Long or Short, Jakes or Jills, Dollars or Euros, why is it necessary for them to own jets ,million dollar homes with gold plated toilet seats, and several expensive fancy cars?

Someone who works at a bank once told me that some black ministers have accounts at her branch, and the amount of money they deposit in their private accounts every Monday morning is scandalous. So many are fooled by the prosperity preaching rather than Christianity, because that is what they want to hear. I am by no means suggesting that you should not tithe. Only that financial and economic empowerment is not the exclusive right of ministers but should also be extended to their congregation. Furthermore, you should be going to church to receive spiritual empowerment. Can you imagine Jesus being on earth today and having an ATM installed in his church, or asking people for their W2s before becoming members? I certainly don't think so.

Unlike President Reagan, I do not believe that anyone, with the exception of Jesus Christ is worthy of touching the face of God, but when the roll is called up yonder, if you are fortunate enough to be there, then maybe, just maybe, God may touch your face. Let me leave you with this thought.

President Kennedy once said,

"Ask not, what your country can do for you. Ask what you can do for your country".

I say,

"Stop asking President Obama what he's doing for you, and ask what you can do to help him become one of the greatest Presidents of all time, if not the greatest"

"YES YOU CAN!"

Chapter 35

MEXICANS

IT'S BEEN SAID that you are now the largest minority group in the United States, and this gives you a lot of political clout which you should use wisely. In every group, there is the good, the bad, and even the very bad. It's a well known fact that most Mexicans come to the USA to get jobs to support themselves and their families, and live the "American Dream".

I live in a subdivision where new houses are still being built. I witnessed the building of a new house on an empty lot opposite my home, where 95% of the work was done by Mexicans. I have never seen such dedication and team work by any other group of people. This was a basement lot, and I watched them clear it, and mark out the foundation. Caucasians and African Americans delivered the ready mixed concrete, which was leveled by Mexicans, and then I watched in awe as 5 Mexicans framed that two story house in four and a half days. The kitchen cabinets were fitted by Caucasians, but every thing else was done by Mexicans, and in a matter of weeks the house was completed. I call that good, and that applies to most Mexicans.

A Spanish speaking South American told me that when he first arrived in the USA, his main objectives were to get a job, and learn to speak English. He worked in the days and attended English classes at nights. His first job was with a Mexican painting subcontractor, and he was the only non-Mexican in the crew of about 10 painters. However, he had to leave the job when he found out that two of his boss's rules were that they were only allowed to speak Spanish, and eat at Mexican restaurants. I call that bad and hope it applies to a small minority.

Naturally, the very bad is what is reported in the news. This includes murder, robbery, and drug related crimes, which I'm sure applies to a small minority.

I will ask the same question that Senator Reid asked,

"How can anyone from the Hispanic community be a Republican"?

All you have to do is remember the anti-Mexican comments and behavior of xenophobics like McCain, Brewer, and Angle, who speak for the majority of their Republican colleagues, to know that you shouldn't be one. Now that your votes can make a difference, I implore you to use them wisely.

Chapter 36

DIFFICULT TIMES AHEAD

TOWARDS THE END of the 20th century and the beginning of the 21st century, four very important historical events took place. The 20th century saw the rise of Nelson Mandela from a lifetime in prison, to be the President of once apartheid South Africa, and the fall of the Berlin wall which separated democratic West Germany from communist East Germany. This new century has seen the rise of Barack Obama from a community organizer in Chicago to President of The United States of America, and the fall of Hosni Mubarak, freeing 80 million Egyptians from the pressure of 30 years of his autocratic strong-armed rule. All four events seemed inconceivable just a year before they occurred, which just goes to show that nothing is impossible.

The world in general enthusiastically welcomed these historical events with open minds and hearts, because they were necessary and positive moves that were well overdue. Lives were lost in South Africa during Mandela's fight against apartheid. Lives were lost in Egypt in the fight against Mubarak's tyrannical rule. Lives were lost in Germany, when East Germans tried to escape to freedom in West Germany, lives were lost during the civil rights struggle by Martin Luther King, and sacrifices made by others who paved the way for someone like Barack Obama to become President.

Surely, there were those in each of the countries involved who fought vigorously against those great developments. And right here in America the Republicans are living examples of those who want to thwart the progress of this President and in so doing the progress of America as well. Most of them think of Ronald Reagan as their political god, and aspire to be just like him. They place him on this pedestal and almost worship him because he uttered six words,

"Mr. Gorbachev, tear down these walls!"

This had nothing to do with the eventual removal of the wall several years later.

However I might have been willing to echo that accolade, if only he had uttered another five words when he had the chance to do so,

"Mr. Botha, tear down apartheid!"

Instead he vetoed a bill calling for sanctions against South Africa.

Who were the greater sufferers, the East Germans, or the Black South Africans?

It would be unfair to suggest that all Republicans behave badly, and that all Democrats are well behaved, because there is good and bad in both Parties. But when it comes to bad behavior, Republicans are head and shoulders above Democrats. There were many whites who were against slavery, but they were afraid to voice their opinions for fear of being called "N lovers". Now we have a similar situation where some Republicans disagree with the behavior of people like Rush Limbaugh, Sarah Palin, Neal

Boortz, Sean Hannity, Glen Beck, Michelle Bachman, and all the other like-minded Republicans, but choose to remain silent for fear of being reprimanded by the Party's bullies. No matter how hard they try to avoid it, there comes a time when they slip up and say things that reveal their true feelings.

After the emergence of Sarah Palin in the 2008 Presidential Campaign, she almost immediately went ahead and accused then Senator Obama of "palling" around with terrorists. Instead of being discouraged, she was encouraged, and that was the start of the Republicans incendiary campaign rhetoric against him. This continued throughout the campaign, and got much worse after President Obama's inauguration, because now all the "haters" chimed in. It was open "attack the President" season, so let's look back at some of the things that have been said.

Who said, "President Obama is a racist"?

A Republican

Who said "President Obama is the most corrupt President in history"?

A Republican

Who said President Obama is an idiot?

A Republican

Who said, "We will not retreat, but reload"?

A Republican

Who said, she wanted her constituents to be "armed and dangerous"?

A Republican

Who said, people should "resort to second amendment remedies"? A Republican

Who said, "if ballots don't work bullets will"?

A Republican

Who said, "we have more to fear from health care reform than terrorism"?

A Republican

Who wanted to pay $100.00 to anyone who would punch a Democratic Congressman on his nose?

A Republican.

Who wrestled a woman to the ground and stomped on her head because they disagreed with the banner she was carrying?

Republicans

Who said, "We want our country back"?

Republicans

Now add this to the hateful racist banners and guns seen at Tea Party rallies, all aimed at President Obama, and tell me there is nothing wrong with that picture. If the young man who went to a political meeting at a Safeway supermarket in Tucson, Arizona where he killed six people, and injured thirteen, is mentally disturbed, then the young, old and middle aged Republicans who spout their vitriolic rhetoric that injures and sometimes kills the minds of so many Americans must be regarded as intellectually disturbed, intellectually delusional, and intellectually dishonest. They should probably seek help from someone like Dr. Phil, if he would be willing to tackle an almost impossible job. No one has linked the Tucson shooting to the hateful behavior of these Republicans, but if you deliberately but unnecessarily pour gasoline on a building and someone puts a match to it, then surely you must accept some of the blame for its burning.

Violent rhetoric can lead to violent action by unbalanced people. All they need is a little nudge to go over the edge, and so it's not surprising, but really amusing to hear the guilty parties say they are shocked at what took place in Tucson, when what they really mean is, they are shocked at who got shot, and who didn't. To top it all, they want to be absolved from any blame.

Let's pause for a while and assume that Barack Obama had targeted a Republican's district in the same way that the Ernor did, and a Republican Congresswoman got shot.

Now sit back, close your eyes and let your minds' eyes and ears look at and listen to the devastating assault on him by cackling Palin, depraved Bachman, namby-pamby Beck, hanky-panky Hannity, braggadocio Boortz, and egotistical Limbaugh to name a few. Think how well that would go down with their supporters.

Now open your eyes to the reality that neither knowledgeable Chris Matthews, assertive Ed Schultz, factual Keith Olberman, definitive Rachel Maddow, nor authoritative Lawrence O'Donnell to name a few, blamed the "Ernor" for that terrible incident.

See the difference?

She in fact, maybe because of a guilty conscience, directed the blame towards herself.

As with all the other incidents of killings and injuries caused by guns in the past, this one will be talked about for awhile. Nothing will be done about gun control, it will soon be forgotten, it will be back to business as usual, until the next tragedy occurs, and the recurring decimal reappears. The fanatical fight by the right to bear arms has nothing to do with Constitution Rights, but everything to do with "MONEY".

To add insult to injury come the statement from the Ernor that should completely insult the intelligence of even her most ardent supporters when she said,

"When we take up our arms, we are talking about our votes."

How pathetic? Yet she gets buyers for her crap, and once again laughs all the way to the bank.

It's going to be very difficult for Democrats to do business with Republicans, especially after what took place in the 2010 November election. Voters armed with the relentless barrage of incendiary rhetoric they received from the Republican and Tea Parties, frustrated by the economic decline, and influenced by their own impatience, went to the polls and caused a political earthquake that shook the very foundation of the Democratic Party. The ensuing tsunami is now being felt as the sea of Republican and Tea Party Politicians wreak havoc across the nation, and the helpless inhabitants watch their country catapult in a downward spiral. It will certainly get worse as these Politicians continue to carry out the wishes of their wealthy bosses, at the expense of poor and middle class Americans. It will only get better if voters do not again allow themselves to be duped into buying the Good Crap Republicans so proudly sell, and use their votes wisely at the next election.

Now that they have this uncontrollable majority in the House, they want to repeal the health care bill, scrap the board of education, privatize social security, and destroy Medicare and Medicaid, destroy the Unions, and take away the collective bargaining rights of workers. They defended oil companies during the BP oil disaster in the Gulf, and they defended big banks during the debate dealing with financial reform.

"So what are the chances of Democrats finding common ground with Republicans?"

To achieve any success, Democrats would have to borrow the Republican dictionary, and be willing to accept their definitions of certain words and phrases. For instance,

Negotiate: Reaching a settlement by conferring with ourselves. "Heads' Republicans win, "Tails" Democrats lose

Compromise: Our way or the highway

Great Americans: Those who agree with everything we say or do

The American People: Millionaires and billionaires

Investment: Excessive spending

This would be a very difficult undertaking

The President is prepared to meet them half way in an effort to move the country forward. As a matter of fact he has gone more than half way, while they have not yet left their starting point.

EPILOGUE

THIS IS MY FIFTEENTH YEAR IN ATLANTA. It took me a long time to make some of the necessary adjustments, but as this may be my final destination, I will continue to press on. America is only one of many great countries on this great planet called Earth. There are people from most, if not all of these other countries living here in the USA, making it one of the most diverse countries in the world, but it's predominantly white, and some, a minority thankfully, believe they are supreme, and the country belongs to them alone. Hopefully in time they will disappear just like the dinosaurs, because that is the only way to peaceful co-existence among all Americans.

Why should it matter here in America where religious freedom is practiced, if you are a Catholic, Protestant or Jew worshipping God, a Muslim worshipping Allah, a Witness worshipping Jehovah, or a Rastafarian worshipping Jah, when we are in fact worshipping the same supreme-being, but calling him by different names. Why should it matter if you are black, white, brown, red, yellow or any color, when we have no control over our birth places or birth parents, and we already have enough problems worrying about the color green? We tend to forget a very basic and important fact, one that should unite all the peoples of the world, and that is,

"We are all of one race, the Human Race".

Now that you have seen laid out before you how one statement can be insignificant, but when compiled together it shows how poisonous and dangerous the rhetoric can be. Will you continue to buy Good Crap, or will you come to the realization that crap is crap no matter how well it's gift wrapped or who delivers it?

I try very hard to be optimistic about the future, and with Barack Obama as President, optimism seems an easy option. But with this current Republican opposition, pessimism steps in and puts me in a dilemma.

Good will always triumph over evil, and so should optimism over pessimism so, for now, let's just say...

I'm a "Pessimistic Optimist"

REFERENCES

CNN

MSNBC

GOOGLE

WSB RADIO

www.ingramcontent.com/pod-product-compliance
Lightning Source LLC
Chambersburg PA
CBHW061311280526
45784CB00002B/957